11/13

Time Management
for Department Chairs

Jossey-Bass Resources for Department Chairs

Books

Jeffrey L. Buller, *Academic Leadership Day by Day: Small Steps That Lead to Great Success*

Jeffrey L. Buller, *The Essential Department Chair: A Practical Guide to College Administration*

Don Chu, *The Department Chair Primer: Leading and Managing Academic Departments*

Robert E. Cipriano, *Facilitating a Collegial Department in Higher Education: Strategies for Success*

Christian K. Hansen, *Time Management for Department Chairs*

Mary Lou Higgerson, *Communication Skills for Department Chairs*

Mary Lou Higgerson and Teddi A. Joyce, *Effective Leadership Communication: A Guide for Department Chairs and Deans for Managing Difficult Situations and People*

Daryl Leaming, *Academic Leadership: A Practical Guide to Chairing the Department, Second Edition*

Daryl Leaming, *Managing People: A Guide for Department Chairs and Deans*

Jon Wergin, *Departments That Work: Building and Sustaining Cultures of Excellence in Academic Programs*

Dan Wheeler et al., *The Department Chair's Handbook, Second Edition*

Journal

The Department Chair

Online Resources

Visit www.departmentchairs.org for information on online seminars, articles, book excerpts, and other resources tailored especially for department chairs.

Time Management for Department Chairs

Christian K. Hansen

JOSSEY-BASS
A Wiley Imprint
www.josseybass.com

Published by Jossey-Bass
A Wiley Imprint
989 Market Street, San Francisco, CA 94103-1741—www.josseybass.com

Readers should be aware that Internet Web sites offered as citations and/or sources for further information may have changed or disappeared between the time this was written and when it is read.

Limit of Liability/Disclaimer of Warranty: While the publisher and author have used their best efforts in preparing this book, they make no representations or warranties with respect to the accuracy or completeness of the contents of this book and specifically disclaim any implied warranties of merchantability or fitness for a particular purpose. No warranty may be created or extended by sales representatives or written sales materials. The advice and strategies contained herein may not be suitable for your situation. You should consult with a professional where appropriate. Neither the publisher nor author shall be liable for any loss of profit or any other commercial damages, including but not limited to special, incidental, consequential, or other damages.

Jossey-Bass books and products are available through most bookstores. To contact Jossey-Bass directly call our Customer Care Department within the U.S. at 800-956-7739, outside the U.S. at 317-572-3986, or fax 317-572-4002.

Jossey-Bass also publishes its books in a variety of electronic formats. Some content that appears in print may not be available in electronic books.

Library of Congress Cataloging-in-Publication Data

Hansen, Christian K.
  Time management for department chairs / Christian K. Hansen.
       p. cm. – (Jossey-Bass resources for department chairs)
  Summary: "In this concise, highly practical book, Christian Hansen draws on his years of research on time management for department chairs. He shows department chairs how to set priorities, create a time budget and log, harness technology to assist in time management, and make self-care a priority. As a handy paperback, this book is designed to be an easy-to-access resource that will not only make department chairs' jobs easier but will also help them to manage stress and prevent burnout." – Provided by publisher.
  Includes bibliographical references and index.
  ISBN 978-0-470-76901-0 (pbk.); 978-1-118-08724-4 (ebk); 978-1-118-08725-1(ebk); 978-1-118-08726-8(ebk);
  1. College department heads.   2. Universities and colleges–Administration.
  3. Time management.   I. Title.
  LB2341.H3217 2011
  378.1'01–dc22

                                                                        2011011121

Printed in the United States of America
FIRST EDITION
PB Printing   10 9 8 7 6 5 4 3 2 1

Contents

The Author

Christian K. Hansen is associate dean of computing and engineering sciences in the College of Science, Health and Engineering at Eastern Washington University (EWU). He also holds an appointment as professor in the Department of Mathematics and served as the department chair from 2001 to 2009. Before joining EWU in 1993, he worked as a reliability specialist at the International Telecommunications Satellite Organization (INTELSAT) in Washington, D.C. He holds a master of science degree in electrical engineering and a doctorate in statistics from the Technical University of Denmark.

After publishing more than two dozen scientific articles within his technical discipline, Hansen has recently focused much of his research on time management and academic leadership. He has led several workshops for department chairs, including presentations at the Academic Chairpersons Conference and the Jossey-Bass Department Chair Leadership Institute. A long-time volunteer with the IEEE, he has served in numerous leadership positions, including vice-president for publications, secretary, newsletter editor, and treasurer of the IEEE Reliability Society. He and his wife, Kelly, an elementary school teacher, have three teenage children living at home.

Acknowledgments

I would like to acknowledge with gratitude and appreciation the individuals who most positively influenced me during the creation of this book:

My wife, Kelly, my son, Jonathan, and my stepdaughters, Kaitlyn and Amanda, for their love and patience during this project. The privilege of spending time with them has been the greatest reward for learning to manage time wisely.

My mother, Birgit, and late father, Carl Evald, for their life-long encouragement and guidance, always leading me to seek my highest potential.

My sister, Ida, and brother, Axel, for their mentorship and many rewarding conversations over the course of my life.

My colleagues in the Department of Mathematics. Without their collegiality and the uninterrupted time given to me during my sabbatical in the fall of 2009, this project would not have been possible.

Two fine deans I have had the pleasure of working with, Dean Emeritus Ray Soltero and Dean Judd Case. Without their leadership and mentorship, I would have never survived eight years as department chair.

The editorial staff at Jossey-Bass, in particular Executive Editor Sheryl Fullerton, for her support and enthusiasm for this project.

Three external reviewers—Christine Licata, N. Douglass Lees, and Jeffrey Buller—for many thoughtful comments and suggestions that greatly improved the final manuscript of this book.

Above all, I thank God, the creator of time, life, and all the treasures we enjoy, without whom nothing else would have mattered.

C.K.H.

Time Management
for Department Chairs

1

IT'S ABOUT TIME

The Highly Effective Department Chair

> There are no great limits to growth because
> there are no limits of human intelligence,
> imagination, and wonder.
>
> —*Ronald Reagan*

Writing this book took me about 567 hours, including many hours during my sabbatical in the fall of 2009 studying the literature on time management and department chair leadership and writing many pages of content that did not make it into the final version of the book. Prior to that I spent eight years as chair of the Department of Mathematics at Eastern Washington University, during which time I spent an estimated 2,147 hours reading and replying to e-mails, writing memos, and doing other routine office tasks, 954 hours preparing and revising course schedules, and 221 hours dealing with student complaints, all of which gave inspiration for many anecdotes and case studies presented in this book. I don't have an accurate count of the number of times my colleagues or students interrupted me in the middle of an important task or the number of hours I wasted completing tasks that turned out to have no meaningful payoff. Yet if you read at the same rate as I do, you will be able to read this book and learn what I learned during this time in less than three hours.

Like most department chairs, I spent most of my professional career prior to accepting this position teaching college classes, writing research articles in my field of specialization, and serving in numerous service functions, none of which had any relevance to the skills needed to be a successful department chair. Among those skills, I found time management to be the most crucial one. A few years into my first term as chair, as a recovering workaholic and urgency addict, I became a self-professed student of time management. Through studying, presenting workshops on the topic at professional meetings, and writing this book and several articles (Hansen, 2007, 2008, 2009b), I have remained a student of this subject rather than an expert.

From this perspective, this book is different from any other time management book available. Nearly all such books are written by experts in the field, authors who have given work-shops and seminars to thousands of professionals around the world and appeared frequently on prime-time network television. With the exception of one time management book (Whisenhunt, 1987), all books on time management referenced in this book are written by someone who has never served in an academic leadership position. Authors like Alan Lakein, Alec MacKenzie, and Stephen Covey have all made significant contributions to the foundation of time management, but their books are written with the private business professional in mind. This is not a coincidence, for this audience makes up the vast majority of today's workforce. My book is written for a much smaller audi-ence, the audience of department chairs. With respect to articles on time management specifically written for department chairs, only a handful are cited in this book, including Crandell (2005), Hecht (2005), and Hedges (2003). Here are some of the ways in which department chairs' time management problems differ from those of business professionals:

- More complex reporting structures (spider web organization rather than tree organization)
- Different measures of productivity (student preparation for careers, intellectual property, and service to the community rather than revenue generation)

- More complex hiring structures and reduced mobility among employees
- Workloads defined by functions rather than time commitments
- More focus on people than on things (85 to 90 percent of university budgets are allocated to people)

This book offers no new fundamental theory of time management. It does not attempt to introduce a fifth generation of time management or a ninth habit of effectiveness. It offers practical advice on how to effectively lead an academic unit and manage its resources, with a focus on making the most effective use of time for the department chair and everyone with whom he or she interacts.

The Need for Balance

Everyone knows that if we had more time, we could do more. But we cannot get more time because we already have all the time there is. Time management is not about creating more time but rather about making the best use of the time we have. Much of what is discussed in this book is about creating balance: balancing chair and faculty workload, balancing time spent on the various duties of the chair position, balancing productivity with product capability, balancing work and family, and so on. Vilfredo Pareto's 80/20 principle (Koch, 1998) indicates that imbalance rather than balance is the natural state of affairs. Thus with time management, we seek to create balance by working against our natural tendency to create imbalance.

You Are Already Doing a Great Job

In spite of the complex nature of the job, new department chairs usually receive inadequate training, if any at all, before stepping into the position (Chu, 2006; Gmelch and Miskin, 2004). Many new chairs are overwhelmed with the number of demands placed on their time and get buried in paperwork, faculty evaluations, and meetings. My impression from talking to many department chairs and to researchers who have studied the chair profession itself is that in spite of the lack of preparation, the vast majority of chairs are perceived as being successful in their job. This view of the department chair may be biased because most of the ones I have met actively seek to improve themselves by studying the literature and attending conferences for people in their profession. Certainly anyone reading this book would fall within this limited scope. So if you are like most of the department chairs I have met, chances are that you are already doing a great job.

Effective time management skills represent only a small subset of the skills needed to be a successful department chair, including those discussed in the general leadership books for department chairs, such as Buller (2006), Chu (2006), Conway (1996), Gmelch and Miskin (2004), Hecht and colleagues (1999), Leamyng (2007), Lees (2006), and Tucker (1992). It is certainly possible for someone to have good time management skills and yet do a poor job as department chair. More commonly, I have seen department chairs who are doing well in the job *in spite of* poor time management skills. Consider the following comment made by rock legend Alice Cooper in his 2007 book *Alice Cooper, Golf Monster*: "When I think about all the time I wasted drunk, it makes me cringe. There are four albums that I don't even remember writing or recording! I look back at those albums and there are some good songs on them. I would love to rerecord some of those tunes now that I am sober and make them into really great songs. They may have turned out okay, but I know they could have been so much better" (p. 202). Similarly, many department chairs are doing a great job but could be doing an even greater job by overcoming their addiction to urgency, personal disorganization, and stress, and their lack of ability to prioritize. Many department chairs work 50, 60, or more hours a week, sacrificing their personal lives, shortchanging their families, and putting their health at serious risk.

Mastering time management does not imply that hard work can be avoided, and in most cases the job of department chair will require a workweek of more than 40 hours, at least during busy periods. The 80/20 principle suggests that 80 percent of our results are accomplished through only 20 percent of our efforts, but to propose that 80 percent of what a department chair does in a week could be done in one day's hard work is absurd. Nevertheless, the 80/20 principle can be very useful in determining areas where department chairs can improve in their use of time.

Like Alice Cooper, who traded his dangerous addiction to alcohol for healthier addictions to golf and music, you, by learning time management, can trade your addiction to urgency for healthier addictions to results and effectiveness. Applying the methods discussed in this book, you should be able to identify areas in which your use of time is not very effective and make changes that will result in spending more time on the aspects of your job that really matter and eliminating many that don't. You may already be doing a great job, but with effective time management you could be doing even better and make your job more enjoyable.

Personal Time Versus Department Time

Most time management books are written with the individual person in mind. However, considering "personal" time management in isolation leads to the false belief that each individual's time is worth more than everyone else's. A department chair is not only responsible for managing his or her own personal time (at work and at home) but is also responsible for managing "department" time from a more global perspective. Seeing that most tasks are assigned to a department through the department chair, the chair is ultimately responsible for setting priorities not just at the personal level but at the department level as well, especially in light of the fact that the collective department time of all faculty and staff is limited.

Whereas the total sum of individual time is a constant, the total sum of department time varies with the size and composition of the department in terms of faculty and staff. In a small department with only a few faculty and little or no support staff, managing department time is highly correlated with how well a chair manages his or her own personal time. In a large department with perhaps over one hundred faculty members and a large support staff, there is more department time available but also a larger volume of workload to be managed. Managing a large volume of department time can be both easier and more difficult than managing a small volume. It may be easier because the chair has more options to delegate work and thus ease the impact on personal time but more difficult because there is a much higher potential for disaster and magnitude of impact on the chair's personal time if the chair is not effective in delegating tasks and in prioritizing tasks assigned to the department.

Differences in the Department Chair Role

Although many of the examples presented in this book are based on my own environment, I am well aware that the department chair position varies from institution to institution, from discipline to discipline, and with the size and complexity of each department. Consequently, what constitutes priority "chair work" varies a great deal from position to position.

At a two-year institution where most faculty are hired just to teach, the chair is often solely responsible for major administrative tasks, including hiring and evaluating faculty. With often a heavy workload in both teaching and administrative tasks, chairs in two-year institutions have little or no time to devote to strategic planning, curriculum development, or external affairs. At comprehensive universities with a strong emphasis on research, the chair may be far more concerned with the pursuit of external funding for research than at institutions that focus primarily on teaching. The role of the chair also varies between public and private institutions. At private institutions where all funding comes from tuition and investments, the chair may have a stronger role in student recruitment and alumni relationships than at public institutions where a large portion of the budget is provided by the government. Likewise, as public institutions exist at the mercy of taxpayers and hence are more vulnerable to variations in the economy, political lobbying is becoming more and more important for public institutions, perhaps even affecting the role of the department chair.

What appears to be a common factor among institutions of all types is that colleges and universities around the world have adopted much stricter measures of accountability for faculty performance than what was the case even just a decade ago. Department chairs serving as the main intermediaries between faculty and the administration face increasingly harder challenges in their multiple and sometimes conflicting roles as leaders, managers, and scholars. Ironically, as demands for leadership preparation of department chairs have increased, the time and resources available for chairs to pursue the necessary leadership preparation have decreased.

Organization of This Book

The department chair position requires both management skills and leadership skills. Recognizing that both types of skills are crucial to time management, the chapters in Part One are focused on *managing resources* and chapters in Part Two on *working with people* (faculty, students, staff, administrators, and external constituents). Chapter Ten is intended as the capstone of the book, discussing the important topic of achieving overall work-life balance.

Because time is a limited resource for department chairs, the size of this book was kept to a minimum, making the book ideal as an introduction to the subject on time management for this unique audience. Each of the remaining nine chapters concludes with a list of questions and practical tips intended to provide the reader with tools for self-reflection and suggestions for immediate implementation. Each chapter is written in a casual rather than scholarly tone, with the focus on the chair as a practitioner and with case studies and personal reflections incorporated into the text. The intention of the book is to go beyond anecdotal evidence to provide a solid research-based theoretical foundation on which department chairs in virtually all academic environments can rely.

Part One

WORKING WITH LIMITED RESOURCES

2

GETTING TO THE POINT

Managing Your Priorities

> What is important is seldom urgent and what is
> urgent is seldom important.
>
> —*Dwight D. Eisenhower*

Department chairs must be proactive rather than reactive. Ideally, all of their time should be spent leading efforts that support the goals of their department and college, but often they fall into the trap of simply reacting to other people's agendas. Reactive department chairs easily allow others to consume all of their time, and their prioritization of tasks and activities is often based exclusively on urgency, with little or no regard to what is most important in advancing the department's mission. Unfortunately, much of the time management literature published in the 1970s and 1980s promoted this urgency addiction by emphasizing the daily (or other short-term) to-do list as the main tool for time management.

When you plan one day at a time, the urgent items tend to get all of your attention. Important tasks that are not urgent tend to get pushed off until they become urgent, and you quickly find yourself buried in a long list of tasks that are all urgent. Consider the advice of time management expert Alan Lakein, known as the father of the ABC priority system (Lakein, 1973): "Leave [on your list] only what you are committed to starting for five minutes (and possibly finishing) in the next seven days" (p. 41). However, the really important things, as observed by President Eisenhower, are rarely those that need to get done in the next seven days, and those that do are rarely the most important tasks. In this chapter we will talk about how to overcome this urgency addiction and develop a new habit of working on things that are important while spending only a small portion of time on things that are urgent.

Managing Your Master To-Do List

One important step toward overcoming the urgency addiction is to abandon the daily to-do list. This list should be replaced by a single *master to-do list* that identifies all tasks to be performed over the short or long term, including items on your wish list. For the sake of simplicity, the master to-do list will be referred to from this point on simply as the to-do list. The to-do list may include tasks that have been flagged as needing to be done today, but tasks to be done immediately should never be the subject of an isolated list.

Some listed tasks and activities may be parts of larger projects that must be broken into smaller tasks in order to be manageable. For example, your action plan may call for you to teach Math 441 next fall semester. This semester-long activity can be broken into many smaller tasks, each of which can be done in a single day; for example:

- Write course syllabus.
- Assign homework for week 1.
- Review course roster and room assignment.

Some tasks that occur regularly, such as teaching or preparing for your class, are entered on your calendar rather than your to-do list. You may want to group your tasks so that each task is easily identified with a specific category; for example:

- Advising: Call back new prospective student.
- Space Allocation Committee: Review new space requests.
- Personnel: Visit Dr. ABC's 10:00 class.

It is almost impossible never to deviate from the tasks appearing on the to-do list and calendar. However, the percentage of time spent on tasks not on the to-do list and calendar is one measure that separates good time managers from bad. To reduce this percentage, we must first examine the factors that cause us to deviate from our plans and then decide how we are going to either eliminate them or integrate them into our plans.

First Things First

Almost every time management book uses the language of putting "first things first" somewhere in the text; Stephen Covey and his colleagues (1994) even used the phrase as the title of their excellent book. When it comes down to what exactly "putting first things first" means, however, the literature is not in agreement. Here is how the principle is described in *The Time Trap* (MacKenzie, 1997): "Write down the things you have to do tomorrow. Now number those things in order of their real importance. The first thing tomorrow morning, start working on number one and stay with it until it's completed. Then take number two, and don't go any further until it's finished or until you've done as much as you can. Then proceed to number three and so on. If you can't complete everything on your schedule, don't worry. At least you will have taken care of the most important things before getting distracted by items of less importance. The secret is to do this daily" (pp. 41–42).

There are several problems associated with this advice, given by consultant Ivy Lee to Charles Schwab while he was president of Bethlehem Steel. First, as we have already discussed, by only considering the things "you have to do tomorrow," you have limited the list to things that are urgent. At best, you will be doing the most important tasks only among those that are also urgent. Tasks that are important but not urgent will never even make this list. Second, by starting your day by working your number one priority and sticking with only that until it is finished, you will be ignoring scheduled classes and meetings as well as all incoming messages, which presumably would not be reviewed until the list has been completed or at the end of the day. Tasks that truly do need your immediate attention would not be reviewed in time and could turn small problems into big crises. Finally, many advisers seem to believe that every person's energy level is highest in the morning and decreases linearly throughout the day. It is true that some people work best in the morning and should schedule their most demanding activities at that time, but other people work best in the evening and should plan differently. Also, sometimes you may want to set aside a block of time to simply take care of little routine tasks. That may include short tasks such as returning a phone call or two, things that may not be your number one priority but makes sense to be blocked together. Indeed, in the fourth edition of *The Time Trap* (MacKenzie and Nickerson, 2009), the comment was added that "the classic advice that Ivy Lee gave . . . may no longer apply in today's multitasking milieu" (p. 86).

So what is the "first thing" that needs to be done? The question is really, What is the very next thing that needs your attention? Essentially, there are three types of tasks or activities that are competing for your time:

Scheduled activities (calendar)

Unscheduled tasks (to-do list)

Interruptions

Ordinarily, a scheduled activity should take priority over an unscheduled task or activity. If you follow this rule, you can increase the priority of a task or activity by simply scheduling it on your calendar. By their nature, interruptions tend to take precedence over all other tasks and activities regardless of their relative importance. Although you cannot eliminate interruptions altogether, you can greatly reduce their impact on your time by appropriately scheduling time to handle e-mail, phone calls, and drop-in visitors as well as setting aside uninterrupted periods to work on high-priority tasks. Occasionally, an interruption may be of such nature that it justifies canceling or rescheduling an already scheduled activity. This is an individual judgment call, and often it is based on the importance of the interruption and the degree of difficulty you may have rescheduling an activity or the consequence of canceling it.

The to-do list should contain some *proactive* tasks in addition to reactive tasks. Proactive tasks are often self-selected and serve the purpose of handling anticipated future tasks in a more effective manner than waiting for the task to be introduced by someone else. For example, it may be anticipated that from time to time your dean will require you to present a cost analysis based on all courses taught and all faculty resources used in the department, or such an analysis may become part of your justification of a new faculty position later on. A proactive task for your to-do list might therefore involve designating a staff member to work on developing and maintaining a spreadsheet with commonly used cost figures and analyses so that a request from a dean for such data does not catch you off guard.

When working through the to-do list, the following scoring system may be helpful in determining priorities. First, classify each of the competing tasks as follows (Gmelch, 2004):

Importance: A score from 1 to 5 measuring the contribution toward your mission

Urgency: A score from 1 to 5 measuring how urgent the task is

Effort needed: Estimated hours (and other resources) required to complete the task

When placing tasks on your to-do list, you may want to record the due date (if applicable) along with other notes relevant to the task. A due date is of course related to the urgency score; however, a due date alone does not determine the urgency of a task.

If you are using an electronic to-do list (you'll find more on this in Chapter Five), you can easily sort tasks by any variable or category you choose. If you are using an integrated system, you will also be able to drag and drop incoming e-mail into your to-do list and assign importance, urgency, effort needed, due date, and set reminders.

When assigning provisional priorities to the tasks on the to-do list, sort all tasks first by importance (most important first), then by urgency (most urgent first), and finally by effort needed (least demanding first). The rationale for this is that importance should take priority over urgency and, everything else being equal, that tasks requiring little effort should be handled before those that require more effort ("picking the lowest-hanging fruit first"). I call these the *provisional* priorities because no automated process or mathematical formula can substitute for personal judgment. Only you will be able to determine whether a task of importance = 4 and urgency = 5, for example, should be done before another task of importance = 5 and urgency = 1.

During my time as department chair, I adopted the following morning routine:

1. Check calendar.
2. Check voice-mail and e-mail messages.
3. Check to-do list.

Although I generally avoided scheduling meetings early in the morning, I needed to check my calendar first because scheduled tasks take priority over nonscheduled tasks. Voice-mail and e-mail were checked before the to-do list for the obvious reason that new incoming tasks could have high priority and possibly "bump" existing priorities. This exercise of reviewing incoming and existing tasks could usually be done in 15 to 30 minutes. I repeated this exercise in the morning, at midday, and in the afternoon or early evening. In my case, being a frequent commuter, I could check my calendar and messages while riding the bus to and from work.

Scheduling Your Priorities

Some time management experts characterize e-mail, telephone calls, drop-in visitors, and similar interruptions as time wasters. But what would happen if you eliminated these activities altogether? Imagine yourself arriving at the office every morning, closing your door with a "Do Not Disturb" sign posted, unplugging your telephone, turning off your e-mail, and working all day long on the top priorities on your to-do list. You would probably be very productive for a short period, but sooner or later you would be buried under an avalanche of matters left unattended. The truth is that e-mail, phone calls, and many other interruptions are high priorities for you. They are your interface with the world around you, and you simply cannot do your job properly without them. But instead of letting these activities gobble up your whole day or isolating yourself from them completely, you must schedule them along with your other priorities. So you will need to set aside times in your calendar for checking your e-mail and voice-mail and limit yourself to returning calls and answering messages during these specific times. Set aside a specific time each day to answer and return phone calls, and let people know when during the day they can stop by to see you without an appointment. Schedule times during your week to take care of routine but necessary paperwork and office tasks, and block off uninterrupted times to work on high-priority (important but not urgent) tasks on your to-do list. Leave some time slots open in your calendar to make room for requested meetings and appointments, but be sure to schedule *your* priorities first. Covey and colleagues (1994) refer to this process as "putting in the big rocks first." Placing your "big" priorities on your calendar before you allow it to get filled up with meetings and interruptions is like the process of putting rocks and sand into a jar. If you put the sand in first, you will never find room for the big rocks. You might enjoy watching a brief video on this topic (Covey, 2004a).

Scheduling your big priorities rather than simply working down your to-do list one item at a time is another important component in the cure for the urgency addiction. Except during the scheduled e-mail periods or office hours, turn the computer's "you have mail" alert off and forward all phone calls to your secretary, the front desk, or your voice-mail. You might want to give a cell phone number only to people who might need to contact you in an emergency, but don't worry: should a real emergency arise, people will find you.

What If There Is an Emergency?

Sometimes a major crisis or emergency will arise out of the blue. In my years as department chair, I dealt with a few emergencies that would cause me to set aside most other priorities for weeks or more. Early in my first term as chair, a beloved faculty member was killed in an auto accident that claimed the lives of five people associated directly or indirectly with our university. I had news crews from all three local news stations in my office the next morning while I was making arrangements for her classes to be notified and covered for the rest of the term. Less than a year later, another valued faculty member passed away at age forty-six after suffering a sudden heart attack. I experienced several other emergencies that required a 911 call for an ambulance or the dispatching of campus police. But crises do not occur on a daily basis. Department chairs who claim that they spend every day managing crises and putting out fires are just people with urgency addictions, people who live at the mercy of other people's priorities. Other people's crises do not necessarily have to be yours. Your job is not to bail out everyone under the sun, including those who have postponed important tasks until the last minute and now need your help to dig them out of the trouble they have gotten themselves into.

Maintaining the P/PC Balance

Not everything we do at work directly advances the institution toward a stated goal or vision. Activities such as completing faculty evaluations, organizing your office, or reflecting on lessons learned are activities that serve the purpose of maintaining or improving your *ability to produce* rather than the purpose of *producing* itself. Covey (1989) describes the importance of maintaining a proper "P/PC balance," the balance between producing (P) and maintaining production capability (PC). In academia, "production" is usually measured in terms of things like student credit hours and number of peer-reviewed publications, while things like curriculum development, research, and developing and improving campus infrastructure all represent "production capability." We must manage our time such that we increase production in balance with increasing our production capability. During nearly two decades in higher education, I have seen many examples of institutions getting out of P/PC balance, especially during challenging financial times. When facing budget challenges, it is the natural instinct of most higher-level administrators to focus only on P, increasing faculty workloads to cover classes and maintaining student credit hours and tuition revenue generation, while neglecting PC by reducing funding for professional development, information technology, and so on. I have also seen opposite examples of P/PC imbalance, especially at the personal level, when faculty members build PC without increasing P—for example, by spending an excessive amount of time on research without ever getting an article published or attending workshops without applying their new knowledge.

Lack of P/PC balance is often directly associated with the urgency addiction discussed earlier. Consider the two pyramids shown in Figure 2.1. Pyramid (a) shows a healthy approach to time management. The top two sections represent time devoted to the important productive tasks, with the peak identifying those that are both urgent and important. The bottom part of

Figure 2.1 P/PC Pyramids Depicting "Healthy" and "Unhealthy" Time Management Habits

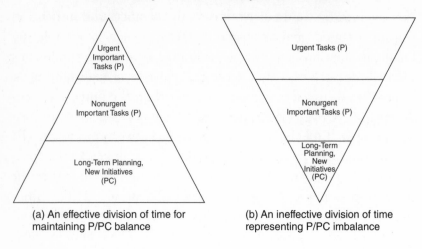

(a) An effective division of time for maintaining P/PC balance

(b) An ineffective division of time representing P/PC imbalance

the pyramid represents time spent on various PC activities, such as long-term planning and new initiatives. Pyramid (b) shows the inverted priorities of people with urgency addictions. Urgent tasks, many of which are not important, take up most of the manager's time, with little left for PC activities.

Questions to Consider and Practical Tips

- Preparing your calendar and to-do list electronically can be a great time saver. If you are not already doing so, spend some time learning how to integrate your calendar and list into a modern electronic integrated system.

- Analyze the content of your current to-do list, and score each item in terms of importance, urgency, and effort needed. For the next week or so, keep an eye on which items are getting crossed off your list. Are the important items getting done, or are you just playing catch-up, dealing with urgent overdue items and ignoring more important matters?

- Consider adding one or more new proactive tasks to your to-do list. If you can, think of tasks that do not require your immediate attention but might ultimately save you or your department time.

- Consider your calendar for the upcoming week. How many of your appointments are reactive (for example, meetings you have felt pressured to attend), and how many are proactive (for example, meetings that you took the initiative to schedule to discuss new strategic initiatives for your department)?

- Consider your personal as well as your department's P/ PC balance. If the appropriate balance does not exist, what can you do to achieve a better balance?

3

THE ART OF ENOUGH

Managing Your Resources

Don't let yesterday use up too much of today.
—*Will Rogers*

Time, money, information, physical resources, and human resources are the five basic resources that must be managed wisely in any organization in order to achieve specific goals. The management of time, at least in principle, is an illusion in that time exists independently of the other four resources and cannot be created, bought, sold, or otherwise manipulated like the other resources (Douglass and Douglass, 1980). Money, by contrast, can be transformed into information, physical resources, and human resources; consequently, time and money are the two resources that department chairs are most concerned about. Although department chairs do not think of themselves as "managing" human resources, these are without question the department's most valuable asset; in fact, typically, 85 to 90 percent of a department's budget is directly tied to human resources. Although faculty cannot be managed in the way other resources can, the chair's leadership skills can influence faculty to perform at their optimal level. (We will discuss this in more detail in Chapters Six through Eight.)

In principle, time and money are not interchangeable, but for practical purposes, many tasks are of such a nature that trade-offs between time and money can be made. For example, we hire assistants to help us perform tasks that we would otherwise have performed ourselves (trading money for time). Or we engage in services that consume our time but generate revenue that will be available for us (trading time for money). Time management is not only about prioritizing tasks and activities but also about making wise trade-offs that effectively utilize our combined resources of time and money.

There are many ways in which time and money are similar and some ways in which the two are fundamentally different. A similar characteristic of time and money is that wasting either one represents a lost opportunity to reach something that is of value to you or your academic unit. Perhaps the biggest difference between time and money is the attitude most people have toward consuming the two resources. All of us, from time to time, make poor financial choices that result in a loss of money (in large or small amounts) that could have been spent better. Most people feel bad about wasting money. Yet the truth is that most of us waste large portions of our own time as well as other people's time and don't feel the least bit bad about it.

One important element in improving your management of time is to ask the following question: Am I making wise choices in trade-offs between time and money at both the professional and the personal level? At the professional level, this mostly translates into deciding which tasks to delegate and which to do yourself. If you choose to do one yourself, you are consuming your time, and if you delegate it, you are consuming your department's financial funds (assuming that you could reduce the hours of your assistant or colleague if you delegated less).

In making good trade-offs between time and money in your job, consider the monetary cost of every task or activity that you choose to do. For example, in deciding whether to have one or two department meetings each month, consider the cost of these meetings (more on this in Chapter Seven). Does the cost of the tasks you are doing reflect an effective use of time and money, or could those resources have been used to greater benefit elsewhere?

Scarcity Versus Abundance Mentality

Do you frequently use phrases like "it's a zero-sum game" or "I can only do so much"? Do you believe that increasing resources for your academic unit is a matter of effective competition or effective cooperation? Take a look at the phrases in Table 3.1, and think about which types of words and phrases are most common in your vocabulary. If you are like most department chairs, you probably associate mostly with the words and phrases on the left side of the table, those common to people with a "scarcity mind-set." Scarcity-minded people think in terms of resources being limited, that there is only so much to go around, and that the only way to increase resources is through competition. Their gain is someone else's loss. Abundance-minded people tend to focus on their potential rather than their limitations. They believe that there is "enough for all of us," and they regard their successful peers as mentors rather than as competitors (Covey, 1989).

But wait a minute, isn't my university's budget fixed, so that if I get something, someone else has to give something up? If you

Table 3.1 Expressions Commonly Used by Leaders Who Think in Terms of Scarcity and Those Who Think in Terms of Abundance

Scarcity Mind-Set	Abundance Mind-Set
Budget restrictions	New source of revenue
Inequity	Unused potential
"There are 'haves' and 'have nots.'"	"We are all very fortunate."
Competition	Cooperation
Zero-sum game	Win-win
Can only do so much	No limit to our potential
Closed system	Open system
Political decision	Rational decision
Beyond my control	Potential to influence

think short-term, maybe so, but not if you think long-term. Suppose you are trying to get funding for a new tenure-track position. Does that mean that another department will have to lose one? Not necessarily. For both public and private institutions, budgets are highly dependent on total enrollment. Moreover, if you have been successful in recruiting more new students for your programs, it is likely that you have also been responsible for increasing enrollment for other departments. Departments, colleges, and universities, as well as state and federal budgets, are all open systems. They can all grow or shrink without doing so at the cost of another unit. Let's now consider two examples involving scarcity- and abundance-minded thinking.

Example 1

At University X, near the end of an academic year, a dean announces at a chairs' meeting that the college has some residual funds that need to be spent on a onetime basis before the end of the fiscal year. The dean asks all department chairs to bring back "wish lists" from their departments related to equipment and classroom technology enhancements for discussion at the next chairs' meeting. One particular department chair, Dr. Z, decides to devote a large portion of his next department meeting to developing such a wish list, putting more items on the list than can be covered by the funding but hoping that his department will at least get funding for its top one or two priorities as what he and his faculty consider their "fair share."

The chairs' meeting that follows turns out to be a disaster. By majority vote, it is decided to create a "master list" that includes all of the proposed items, and each chair is given a number of votes that can be placed on any items of choice. The items that receive the most votes are then funded, up to the point where all funds have been depleted. The chairs of some of the largest departments in the college, including Dr. Z, feel that this process is unfair in that having the same voting power for every department regardless of size is unfavorable to the larger departments. Added to that, many of the small departments are forming alliances to support items of common interest, whereas the largest departments are proposing items of more isolated interest. In the end, a curious application of the 80/20 principle is achieved whereby 80 percent of the funds are given to only 20 percent of the college.

Example 2

At University Y, several chairs and an associate dean from the natural sciences get together to write a STEM (science, technology, engineering, and mathematics) grant proposal. All science departments agree to support a proposal that is aimed at improving the quality of precalculus instruction by having more classes taught by regular mathematics faculty instead of graduate instructors and providing more extensive mentoring and training of the graduate instructors who teach courses. By thinking in terms of abundance rather than scarcity, everyone involved works in synergistic cooperation to write a win-win proposal. The chairs all agree that this project will be of benefit to the students they serve over the long term. For example, if a biology student has a bad experience in mathematics, that will increase the chance that the student will switch majors or even drop out of college completely. Seeing that all science and engineering majors have to take mathematics, a win for the Mathematics Department is a win for everyone.

Let's compare these two scenarios. In Example 1, the scarcity-minded thinking of everyone involved results in substantial feelings of inequity, lack of trust, and polarization between departments. A large dollar amount is spent with more negative impacts than positive. In Example 2, abundance-minded thinking allows everyone to think "outside the box" to achieve an overall win for all. Note that in these examples, scarcity thinking happens even in the process of distributing unanticipated resources, whereas abundance thinking happens even when there are no resources to distribute.

I want to emphasize that being abundance-minded does not mean being in denial or ignorant of the impact that a major challenge, such as a budget reduction, can have on your department's operation. The main difference between scarcity and abundance thinking is that scarcity-minded people tend to see changes as threats and abundance-minded people see them as opportunities. Being abundance-minded does not mean that you have endless capacity to do "more for less." Scarcity- and abundance-minded people alike can do "more for more" and "less for less." There are a number of factors over which you have no control. State budgets for higher education rise and decline with changes in the political climate and the economy. Budgets for private institutions are affected by other factors that you cannot control. A crash of the stock market can significantly lower a private institution's endowment, and in a recession, donations tend to decline and fewer people can afford to send their kids to expensive private institutions.

But being an effective department chair is not just about producing more with your resources. During lean times, your focus should be on protecting your key investments, namely, your valuable faculty and their loyalty. You can't maintain the same production with fewer resources, so you should prioritize by suspending the functions that can most easily be reactivated once resources are restored, along with those that should have been eliminated anyway. Use the lean times to plan your strategy for the good times to come. History shows that good times always follow lean times, so be prepared to present your needs to your dean once resources come back to your school or college. Leaders who are negligent during the good times and panic during lean times are the ones who tend to buy high and sell low. In contrast, those who plan for the good times during the lean times are the ones who buy low and sell high.

How Much Is Your Time Worth?

Much of the time management literature points to the importance of knowing the value of your own time. Figuring out your value is not complicated math. It basically involves dividing the number of hours you work per year into your annual salary. However, there is a slight difference in what an hour of your time is worth to you and what it is worth to your institution. Douglass and Douglass (1980) give detailed instructions for figuring out how much you are costing your institution per hour, taking into account not just salary and benefits but also cost of office space, utilities, secretarial support, professional development, and equipment, and counting as total hours worked only hours during which you are actually producing (that is, subtracting time spent eating lunch, drinking coffee, going to the bathroom, checking your personal e-mail, and so on). If you had to bill your institution for the hours that you actually worked, how many "billable" hours are you producing each year? Suppose you make $100,000 per year in salary and benefits and you work an estimated 2,000 hours per year. That would result in an hourly rate of $50 per hour. But when you figure in the cost of your secretarial staff, your office space, and other overhead and the percentage of time that you are being productive, it is more likely that your hourly rate is on the order of $200 to $250 (which is closer to the hourly rates charged by professional consultants).

Questions to Consider and Practical Tips

- Compile a list of the major assets among your four tangible resources: money, information, physical resources, and human resources. What proportion of your (financial) budget is associated with each of the other three resources mentioned?

- How much control do you have over each of your tangible resources? For example, what portion of your budget is locked into salaries over which you have no control?

- How much is an hour of your time worth? Add up your salary, benefits, and other work-related expenses paid by your institution, and divide it by the estimated number of hours you work per year.

- How much is an hour of "department time" worth? Based on a calculation similar to the one suggested for your own time, how much does a one-hour meeting involving all your faculty and staff cost your institution?

- Consider the relationship between the time and money that you control at both the personal and the department level. Are you making wise trade-offs between time and money? For example, could you free up time by hiring people to do things that you (or your department) are currently doing? Are there tasks that you (or your department) are currently doing for which the cost is higher than it would be to hire someone else to do them?

- Review the expressions listed in Table 3.1, and circle the ones you use most commonly in your vocabulary as a leader. Do you have a scarcity or abundance mind-set? If you are predominantly scarcity-minded, do you believe that your mind-set limits your imagination in terms of the growth and prosperity of your department?

4

KNOWING WHERE YOU STAND

Analyzing Your Use of Time

> There are a million ways to lose a work day, but
> not even a single way to get one back.
> > —*Tom DeMarco and Timothy Lister*

In this chapter we will look at two important components of time management: time logging and time budgeting. A time log shows how you are using your time. A time budget defines how you *should* be using it. Priorities and resources, as discussed in Chapters Two and Three, should determine both how you plan to use your time and how you actually use it. In an ideal world, you do what you plan to do, so ideally the time log and the time budget should reflect the same distribution of time usage. Even for people with effective time management skills, however, that is rarely the case. There are two primary reasons for this discrepancy. Reason number one is that priorities change—things come up that are more important than the activities you planned, and they change how you use your time. Reason number two is that most people miscalculate how much time activities take. Time budgets are a lot like financial budgets. Unanticipated expenses occur, and we cannot accurately estimate all of our nonrecurring expenses.

Imagine what a university would be like if it did not have a budget. Imagine the chaos that would exist if money was spent arbitrarily at the same rate it was generated. The fact is that your usage of time is equally chaotic if you do not budget it wisely. The more experience you have working with time logs and budgets, the better you will be at avoiding reason number two, by being better at correctly estimating the time needed for regular activities and new projects. As Randy Pausch wisely said, "If you have a plan, you can always change it. However, failing to plan is planning to fail" (Pausch, 2008).

Where Have All the Hours Gone?

Many university administrations and state legislators have attempted to collect data on faculty's use of time in the interest of establishing accountability to taxpayers, donors, and other stakeholders. The problem with most of these studies is that data are self-reported. As a young assistant professor, I was once asked to participate in such a survey. The questionnaire asked about hours I spent teaching, preparing for class, performing service functions, and doing scholarly and research activities. Like everyone else, I had no accurate records, so I "guesstimated" on the high side at about 60 hours per week. Published studies give similar self-reported results based on a larger sample. Some professors in a study by Robinson and Godbey (1999) reported working as much as 90 hours a week, but clearly their data are inflated. In fact, Robinson and Godbey report that for many of the respondents, the total time spent on all activities (including eating and sleeping) add up to more than the actual 168 hours in a week.

Let's face it: nobody is in a position to provide an accurate account of the tasks and activities performed in the past week or how much time each activity took simply out of memory. And nobody wants to be known as a slacker or even someone who "just works 40 hours a week." But how many hours do you *really* work? And more important, what do you *achieve* as result of the hours you put in? The only way to find out is through the use of a time log that records time spent on tasks and activities as they happen. The time log in Exhibit 4.1 represents a typical day at the office for a department chair. As noted by Gmelch and

Miskin (2004), the day of a department chair is characterized by brevity, variety, and fragmentation. Even personal activities such as commuting and eating lunch may be fragmented and mixed with work-related activities. Frequent interruptions break the day into many small pieces and activities that apart from scheduled meetings rarely last more than 10 minutes. In this example, the chair leaves home about 7:00 A.M. and arrives home at 6:00 P.M. If we subtract time spent on personal activities, including half of the commuting time (walking to and from the bus and so on), time spent socializing with friends (non-work-related activities), getting coffee, calling home, and the like, we see that the chair worked approximately nine hours that day, not including time worked in the evening. But how much was accomplished? Only the person recording the time log can answer this question, but seeing that this is a simulated example, let's try to analyze the time log as if it were yours. How many of the phone calls really needed your immediate attention? Could an assistant or a secretary have answered and handled these calls, including the call from the dean, or could they have been directed to your voice-mail and answered in a block after you had collected all the information you needed? One call was from a parent, probably the parent of the student who had a concern about one your professors. Such issues need to be handled promptly, but 15 minutes before your department meeting is not a good time to discuss a sensitive matter with an upset parent. Returning the call to the parent later in the day or setting up a meeting with the student the next day would have been a better solution. What was the nature of your meeting with the dean of graduate studies? Could your graduate program director or a senior faculty member have attended the meeting on your behalf and reported back to you or brought back materials needing your action? What was accomplished during your department meeting? Were there action items that required a face-to-face meeting, or could the meeting have been canceled or shortened? How prepared were you for this meeting? It appears that you were waiting until the last minute to get handouts and agendas prepared and photo-copied, perhaps to the extent that you had to make your own copies because the staff was gone for lunch. Judging from the time log, it looks like there were only three scheduled activities on your calendar: two meetings and an office hour. What would have happened if you had scheduled additional blocks of time to work on important things like the spring course schedule? Could you have blocked out time on your calendar to prepare for your department meeting so that it did not have to wait until the last minute?

Exhibit 4.1 A Diary-Type Time Log

Time	Activity	Time Used	Priority	Comment
7:05	Commute, check calendar, voice-mail, e-mail, to-do list	1:05	1	My best opportunity for uninterrupted work
8:10	Arrive at office Get coffee	0:06	3	
8:16	Return phone call—student	0:05	4	Not important; could be delegated
8:21	Int.: TJ—about student	0:06	1	Important
8:27	Return phone call—student	0:04	4	Not important; could be delegated
8:31	Int.: PC—about travel issue	0:11	3	Routine matter
8:42	Reply to e-mail: misc.	0:21	2	Some issues important
9:03	Office hour: Paperwork	0:10	2	Some issues important
9:13	Visitor: New major	0:08	1	Important
9:21	Office hour: Paperwork	0:05	2	Some issues important
9:26	Visitor: Student—complaint	0:17	1	Important
9:43	Looking for KL (not there)	0:08	4	Should have called
9:51	Leave message for KL	0:02	1	Important
9:53	Leave for meeting	0:08	1	
10:01	Meeting with graduate dean	0:42	1	Meeting started late
10:43	Return to office	0:04	1	
10:47	Int.: TJ—KL looking for me	0:01	4	TJ could have used my calendar

(Cont'd)

Exhibit 4.1 *Cont'd*

Time	Activity	Time Used	Priority	Comment
10:48	Looking for KL (not there)	0:05	4	Wasted time
10:53	Prepare for department meeting	0:05	1	Rushing; should have started sooner
10:58	Int.: Phone call from dean	0:15	4	Got off subject
11:13	E-mail report to dean	0:09	4	Wasted time looking for report; secretary should have handled matter
11:24	Prepare for department meeting	0:10	1	Rushing; should have started sooner
11:34	Int.: Phone call—parent	0:09	2	Should have directed to voice-mail; lacking info to deal with now
11:43	Prepare for department meeting	0:16	1	Rushing; should have started sooner
11:59	Int.: KL—talk about student	0:14	2	Should have set up meeting for later
12:13	Prepare for department meeting	0:28	1	Rushing; should have started sooner
12:41	Eat lunch	0:05	1	Never enough time for this
12:46	Int.: Phone call—student	0:03	4	Routine matter; could have been handled by front desk
12:49	Eat lunch	0:06	1	Never enough time for this
12:55	Leave office for meeting	0:05	1	
1:00	Department meeting	1:37	1	Drifted off the agenda; could have been much shorter meeting
2:37	Return to office	0:08	3	Helped clear off tables; student helpers could have done that
2:45	Int.: KC (social)	0:20	4	Could be done over lunch instead
3:05	Int.: Phone call from home	0:06	4	Son forgot his key; need to have a key hidden somewhere
3:11	Check messages	0:16	3	Nothing really important
3:27	Meeting: New major	0:19	1	Wasted time because network was down
3:46	Int.: Phone call—dean's assistant	0:02	4	Dean could not open my attachment

Exhibit 4.1 *Cont'd*

Time	Activity	Time Used	Priority	Comment
3:48	E-mail report to dean (again)	0:07	4	Converted document and sent it again; secretary could have handled
3:55	Reply to e-mail	0:08	2	Professional activity matter
4:03	Int.: Student with schedule conflict	0:08	2	This happens frequently; need to coordinate schedules with other departments
4:11	Finish reply to e-mail	0:12	2	
4:23	Work on spring schedule	0:08	1	Important; should have started sooner
4:31	Int.: Phone call—student	0:06	4	Routine matter; could have been handled by front desk
4:37	Work on spring schedule	0:05	1	Important; should have started sooner
4:42	Int.: HJ (social)	0:09	4	Could be done over lunch instead
4:51	Get ready to leave to catch bus	0:12	1	
5:03	Commute, check calendar, check messages, analyze time log	1:02	2	What did I accomplish today?
6:05	Arrive home			Exhausted!

Note: Int. = interruption.

As you analyze your time log, especially if collected over a week or two, you will discover habits you have that are preventing you from getting things done in a timely manner, as well as how many hours each day are being wasted. Some of these habits can be difficult to change. Getting your faculty and staff used to the fact that you need to schedule periods on your calendar when you do not want to be disturbed must be achieved with caution. You will need to convince your faculty of the benefits of your being able to accomplish your goals rather than leaving them with the impression that you are unavailable or unwilling to help those who rely on you. Training your staff to handle phone calls and maintain archives of reports and other documents will require some investment of time. And delegating someone else to attend meetings on your behalf, especially those with an administrator of higher rank, likewise, must be done with caution. These issues will be discussed further in Chapters Six through Eight.

Time logs are commonly recorded using one of three forms. The diary-type log is shown in Exhibit 4.1. This format provides a lot of information but is rather time consuming to complete, and it requires additional time for analyzing how much time is used on each task or activity. In fact, the simulated time log in the exhibit omits the time required to record the entries, which can add up. The diary-type time log is recommended for short periods—a few days to a week—when you wish to uncover patterns of interruptions and habits (time wasters) that may need your attention. For time logs compiled over a longer period—say, the course of a semester or an academic year—the account-type log, shown in Exhibit 4.2, is much easier to manage. This type of log is best managed using a spreadsheet. It requires some time to set up, but once the spreadsheet has been prepared, it can be managed in a matter of 10 to 15 minutes a day. In this format, activities are divided into a series of categories ("accounts"). The time spent on each category is tracked throughout the day in the same fashion that lawyers and consultants use when charging their time to a particular client account. Exhibit 4.2 uses the same data as Exhibit 4.1, but for convenience, times are rounded to the nearest 15 minutes (0.25 hour). Time spent in the office on personal matters, such as a phone call home or non-work-related socializing, is assigned to the "all other" account and is not counted in the work hour total. Finally, the grid-type log shown in Exhibit 4.3 records the same information as the account-type log but is more convenient to use when recording data by hand as it involves merely identifying the predominant category for each 15-minute segment of the day.

Exhibit 4.2 An Account-Type Time Log

Tasks and Activities	Hours
Work:	
Miscellaneous Office Work	
Phone/E-Mail/Memos/Other	2.25
Organizing Office/Filing/Computer	
Budget and Planning	
Scheduling	0.50
Budget	
Workload	
Strategic Plan/Policies and Procedures	
Daily Priorities/Time Management	0.25
Committees/Meetings	
Department Business	3.00
Dean/College Business	0.50
University Business	0.75
Personnel/Staff Evaluation/Awards	
Teaching, Advising, and Mentoring	
Preparing for Class/Grading	
Teaching	
Advising	0.50
Student Complaints	1.00
Observing Class/Mentoring	

(Cont'd)

Exhibit 4.2 Cont'd

Tasks and Activities	Hours
Outreach and Events Faculty/Staff/Recruitment Community Outreach Network/Businesses Fundraising Student/Recruitment/Awards Social/Receptions/Events	
Research/Professional Activities Investigations/Research Reading/Writing Articles Colloquia/Conferences Professional Organizations Grant Applications	0.25
Other Sick Time/Doctor's Appointments	
Home + Commute: Commute Exercise All Other	1.00 14.00
TOTAL Work Hours: TOTAL Hours:	9.00 24.00

Exhibit 4.3 A Grid-Type Time Log

Work: *Miscellaneous Office Work*	7–8 A.M.				8–9 A.M.				9–10 A.M.				10–11 A.M.				11 A.M.–12 NOON			
Phone/E-Mail /Memos/Other		x	x		x	x		x	x											
Organizing Office/Filing/ Computer																				
Budget and Planning																				
Scheduling																				
Budget																				
Workload																				
Strategic Plan/Policies and Procedures																				
Daily Priorities/Time Management																				
Committees/Meetings																				
Department Business												x				x	x	x		
Dean/College Business														x						
University Business													x	x	x					
Personnel/Staff Evaluation/ Awards																				
Teaching, Advising, and Mentoring																				
Preparing for Class/Grading																				
Teaching																				
Advising						x			x											
Student Complaints											x									x
Observing Class/Mentoring																				

(Cont'd)

Exhibit 4.3: *Cont'd*

	7–8 A.M.	8–9 A.M.	9–10 A.M.	10–11 A.M.	11 A.M.– 12 NOON
Outreach and Events					
Faculty/Staff/Recruitment					
Community Outreach					
Network/Businesses					
Fundraising					
Student/Recruitment/Awards					
Social/Receptions/Events					
Research/Professional Activities					
Investigations/Research					
Reading/Writing Articles					
Colloquia/Conferences					
Professional Organizations					
Grant Applications					
Other					
Sick Time/Doctor's Appointments					
Home + Commute:					
Commute	x x				
Exercise					
All Other					

Budgeting Your Time

Budgeting time is analogous to budgeting income and expenses in a financial budget. Like a financial budget, a time budget must be balanced; that is, the total time we plan to use must equal the total time we have available. In developing a financial budget, we must plan both income and expenses, both of which are sometimes variable and unknown. A time budget is somewhat simpler because the time we have available is fixed, 24 hours a day, 7 days a week, 15 weeks in a semester. Here we only need to consider how we are going to divide the available time among all the tasks and activities that are competing for it.

The intent is to allocate time to the activities relative to their importance to you or your department. A time budget does not necessarily need to estimate in detail how long each individual task will take. Rather, a time budget allocates the total time available collectively to perform tasks and activities of a certain type over a given period. Not knowing how long each activity will last, we don't know how many activities we will be able to perform, only that we are placing a cap on how much total time we will spend for the period considered. In budgeting time for a particular project, data from time logs previously recorded can be useful. As with financial budgets, we may end up spending more or less than we budgeted on a given activity, but overall we cannot end up with a surplus or deficit. If we spend more or less time than budgeted on one item, one or more other items will have to make up the difference. When creating your initial time allocations, consider the following principle, commonly known as Parkinson's Law (Parkinson, 1955): "Work expands so as to fill time available for its completion." The essence of this principle if that if we do not plan carefully how to spend our time, it naturally gets used up on unimportant trivial tasks. This law is the foundation of the "big rocks" principle discussed in Chapter Two. Once we have put in the "big rocks," the "sand" will naturally fill all of the remaining space.

To illustrate the time-budgeting process, consider again the department chair whose daily time usage was recorded in Exhibits 4.1 through 4.3 (for the sake of this example, we will refer to the chair as "he"). Although a snapshot of a single day is not representative of how he spends his time throughout an entire semester, there are numerous indicators that suggest that this chair is more reactive than proactive and that time is being spent with little regard to what is important. In order to change this, how should he go about planning his time for a period of, say, one semester? Suppose this chair teaches one course this semester that meets four hours a week and requires another eight hours in preparation, grading, and developing new course materials. His other priorities for the semester include filling a vacant faculty position and completing a proposal for a new graduate program (in a discipline within the core of his specialty). Three junior faculty members are being evaluated for tenure and promotion this year, and even though the letters of recommendation are not due until early next semester, he wants to get an early look at each of the promotion files and also complete his class observations for each faculty member. Time permitting, he would also like to get started on the department's strategic plan, which is due at the end of the following semester. As part of his professional goals for the semester, he serves on the board of directors of a professional society and is scheduled to present a paper at a conference next summer. As always, he needs to allocate time to manage the schedule for upcoming semesters, advise new and current students, and attend to other recurring department and university business matters.

A sample time budget is shown in Exhibit 4.4. This budget uses the same categories as Exhibits 4.2 and 4.3, but with estimated daily time allotments shown separately for instruction days and noninstruction days. Some allotments are most easily figured on a daily basis; for example, teaching a 4-credit course would require 0.8 hour daily teaching, on average. Other activities may be better figured on a semester basis—for example, time

Exhibit 4.4 Time Budget for a 15-Week Semester (with Three Holidays)

	Instruction Days	Noninstruction Days	Total Semester	Average Weekly
Number of days:	72	33	105	
Work:				
Miscellaneous Office Work				
Phone/E-Mail/ Memos/Other	1.25	0.25	98.25	6.55
Organizing Office/ Filing/Computer	0.15		10.80	0.72
Budget and Planning				
Scheduling	0.20		14.40	0.96
Budget	0.10		7.20	0.48
Workload	0.10		7.20	0.48
Strategic Plan/ Policies and Procedures	0.30		21.60	1.44
Daily Priorities/Time Management	0.25		18.00	1.20
Committees/Meetings				
Department Business	1.00		72.00	4.80
Dean/College Business	0.20		14.40	0.96
University Business	0.20		14.40	0.96
Personnel/Staff Evaluation/Awards	0.50		36.00	3.40
Teaching, Advising, and Mentoring				
Preparing for Class/ Grading	1.15	1.00	115.80	7.72

(Cont'd)

Exhibit 4.4 *Cont'd*

	Instruction Days	Noninstruction Days	Total Semester	Average Weekly
Teaching	0.80		57.60	3.84
Advising	0.40		28.80	1.92
Student Complaints	0.25		18.00	1.20
Observing Class/ Mentoring	0.20		14.40	0.96
Outreach and Events				
Faculty/Staff/ Recruitment	0.80		57.60	3.84
Community Outreach	0.20		14.40	0.96
Network/Businesses	0.10		7.20	0.48
Fundraising	0.10		7.20	0.48
Student/Recruitment/ Awards	0.10		7.20	0.48
Social/Receptions/ Events	0.10	0.10	10.50	0.70
Research/Professional Activities				
Investigations/ Research		0.10	3.30	0.22
Reading/Writing Articles	0.20	0.20	21.00	1.40
Colloquia/ Conferences	0.10	0.10	10.50	0.70
Professional Organizations	0.10	0.20	13.80	0.92
Grant Applications	0.05	0.05	5.25	0.35
Other				
Sick Time/ Doctor's Appointments	0.10		7.20	0.48

Exhibit 4.4 *Cont'd*

	Instruction Days	*Noninstruction Days*	*Total Semester*	*Average Weekly*
Home + Commute:				
Commute	1.00		72.00	4.80
Exercise	0.50	0.50	52.50	3.50
All Other	13.50	21.50	1,681.50	112.10
TOTAL Work Hours:	9.00	2.00	714.00	47.60
TOTAL Hours:	24.00	24.00		

needed to work on the strategic plan, 20 hours, which amounts to about 0.3 hour daily (rounded). Activities such as checking e-mail, organizing the office, and performing routine office tasks get allocated time based on what is left when all the "big rock" activities have been allocated their time. This chair plans to work an average of nine hours daily for each regular workday (instruction day) and two hours daily on weekends, holidays, and other noninstruction days, with time on the latter reserved primarily for class preparation and professional activities. The non-instruction day time slots are obviously the chair's best chance for working uninterrupted, so that needs to be considered in the planning process.

As you plan your time budget for a quarter or semester, keep in mind that the categories for the time budget (and the time log) can and should be customized to your unique responsibilities. As discussed in Chapter One, what is considered important "chair work" varies greatly from one chair position to another. Also, some people prefer more detail in this budget than others. With more detail, the recording process gets more time-consuming but also more revealing of a person's use of time. The categories must be chosen wisely so that there is just enough detail to distinguish the activities you wish to promote from those you wish to limit. Hence some time allocations may be interpreted as a "maximum" while others may be interpreted as a "minimum." For example, time allocated for e-mail and routine office stuff should be considered a maximum, whereas time allocated to research and professional activities should be considered a minimum. Then if you end up spending less time than planned on e-mail and routine office stuff and more time than planned on reading and writing research articles, you would consider that a plus. For the same reason, I recommend not using generic categories such as "meetings" or "travel." Time spent in meetings and travel should be recorded under the particular function served. For example, a department meeting is "department business," whereas a meeting with a prospective donor is "fundraising." Travel to a conference should be recorded under "attending conferences," and travel to teach at an off-site location should be recorded under "preparing for class." With today's technology, time spent in airports and in airplanes can be usefully devoted to a variety of purposes, and that time should be recorded accordingly. It is debatable whether commuting time should be considered in the same fashion. It could easily be argued that commuting is a work function because you would not be doing it if you were not working. I choose to count commuting time as personal time except for the time I am actually performing work functions, such as checking my e-mail or calendar. Conversely, if I am driving to campus on a Saturday to attend a required work function, I would consider time spent on the relevant work category from the minute I leave home until the minute I return. Keep in mind, however, that time budgeting and time logging data are intended exclusively for your own use, so you can approach them in any way that makes sense to you.

The time budget shown in Exhibit 4.4 does not include details on personal activities such as spending time with the family. These can be included as additional categories if you choose, and this may indeed help you use your personal time as effectively as your work time.

Preparing for the Week Ahead

As a department chair, remember that you are in control of your calendar. Of course, there are required activities that you must schedule on your calendar, such as regular chairs meetings and classes you teach, but for the most part, you have control over what goes on your calendar. If you are using a networked calendar, you may want to authorize your secretary to schedule appointments on your behalf, but the secretary should schedule appointments only in the blocks that you have designated as open. Remember Parkinson's Law. If you don't take control of your calendar, it will gradually get filled based on other people's priorities, not yours.

So it is important to take some time to plan your calendar for the upcoming week, perhaps every Friday afternoon or Sunday evening. To begin preparing your calendar, start with the items that are least flexible: your class times, committee meetings already agreed on, planned travel, and so on. Next block out periods for open office hours as well as quiet times to work on specific projects and blocks for exercise if you do that during the day. These blocks should be chosen carefully. Consider your personal energy cycles. Quiet time blocks should be chosen when your energy is at its highest, while blocks for open office hours and routine work should be scheduled when your energy is lowest. You also need to consider the needs of others; for example, there may be times during the day that would be difficult to claim as uninterrupted time, and scheduling open office hours from 5:00 to 6:00 P.M. would probably not be regarded favorably by your students and colleagues. Blocks can be moved around later, and you may even decide to allow your secretary to do that. Finally, you will need to leave enough open space in your calendar to accommodate the needs for legitimate requests for meetings and appointments that will naturally arise. Exhibit 4.5 is an example of a weekly calendar for the department chair featured earlier in this chapter. At first glance, this looks like a packed calendar,

Exhibit 4.5 Sample Weekly Calendar

	Monday	Tuesday	Wednesday	Thursday	Friday	Saturday	Sunday
7:00	Commute/Check E-mail/Calendar	Commute/Check E-mail/Calendar	Commute/Check E-mail/Calendar	Drive to work Check E-mail/ Calendar	Commute/Check E-mail/Calendar		
8:00	Prepare for Class			Prepare for Class			
9:00	Teach	Student Appointment Student Appointment	Observe Jerry's class	Teach			Church
10:00		Student Appointment Student Appointment	Meeting with Dean			Meghan's Soccer Game	
11:00	Open Office Hour/ Routine Office Work	Open Office Hour/ Routine Office Work	Open Office Hour/ Routine Office Work	Open Office Hour/ Routine Office Work	Open Office Hour/ Routine Office Work		
12:00	Lunch in Office/ Prepare Meeting	Lunch in Office/ Prepare Office Work	Lunch in Office/ Prepare Meeting	Lunch in Office/ Prepare Meeting	Lunch with Bill	Grade/ Prepare for Class	Golf
1:00	Student Appointment	Student Appointment	Department Meeting	Student Appointment			
					Student Appointment		
2:00	Search Committee Meeting	Work on new graduate program proposal				Home projects/ Maintenance	
3:00	Special Chairs Meeting		Work on Jerry's Promotion/Tenure Letter	Work on new graduate program proposal	Review Candidate Files		
4:00							
		Commute/Check E-mail/Calendar					
5:00	Commute/Check E-mail/Calendar	Early Dinner	Commute/Check E-mail/Calendar	Golf Lesson (5:30)	Commute/Check E-mail/Calendar		
Evening	Dinner/ Family Time	Jenny's Recital (6:30)	Dinner/ Family Time Grade/Prepare for Class	Dinner/ Family Time	Dinner/ Joey's Football Game (7:00)	Dinner with Lisa	Read articles/ Review priorities for next week

but a closer examination reveals that there is a lot of flexibility built in. The "big rocks" have been put in first, but there are still plenty of open spaces on this calendar to accommodate additional meeting requests. Parkinson's Law guarantees that each of the open spaces will be filled by the time the week is over, but other people demanding your time will have to pick from the available slots only.

Questions to Consider and Practical Tips

- Try logging your time using the diary format shown in Exhibit 4.1. for a period of one to three days (or a particular time period to which you are willing to commit). Complete the first two columns on the fly and the last three columns at the end of each day. What are the time wasters that are preventing you from focusing on high-priority items? What can you do to reduce or eliminate these time wasters?

- Try logging your time using either the account- or grid-type format shown in Exhibit 4.2 or 4.3, respectively, for a period at least two weeks. Be as general or detailed in your choice of categories as you like. At the end of recording period, compute the percentage of your time spent on each category. How many hours on average did you work per week?

- Create a time budget using the format shown in Exhibit 4.4. Use the same categories as you did in your time log, or modify them as needed. Now log your time for a longer period, such as an academic quarter or semester, and compare time used with time budgeted. Which categories consumed more time than budgeted, and which ones consumed less? Are you satisfied with how you spent your time, or would you budget differently if you were to do it over?

- Plan your calendar for the coming week, as shown in Exhibit 4.5. Be sure to add your "big rocks" to the schedule. Are you comfortable with the amount of remaining time slots for appointments, meetings, and tasks not yet scheduled? Save a copy of your weekly calendar and compare it with your actual calendar at the end of the week. Should you leave more or less open space when planning the calendar for future weeks? How many of your "big rocks" got taken care of as planned, and how many got pushed aside in favor of unanticipated appointments, meetings, and tasks?

5

KEEPING IT ALL STRAIGHT

Getting and Staying Organized

> Science is organized knowledge. Wisdom is
> organized life.
>
> —*Immanuel Kant*

Much has been written on the topic of getting organized, and almost every book on time management has at least one chapter devoted to it (Allen, 2001; Douglass and Douglass, 1980, 1993; Leland and Bailey, 2008; Morgenstern, 2004). Many of these books address issues related to organizing the space in the office as well as the home. Although these are important issues, being organized as a department chair involves a number of additional matters. Perhaps the best way to see the advantages of being organized is to observe the characteristics of a disorganized department chair.

Signs of Disorganization

The disorganized department chair typically exhibits a range of characteristics:

- His office is characterized by a cluttered desk containing stacks of papers needing to be sorted, loose notes from past meetings, and a variety of other items not currently being worked on.

- Her office shelves and bookcases are stuffed with books, reports, and papers in random order. Many textbooks on the shelves are outdated, computer manuals are for software no longer being used, and many reports are more than 10 years old and no longer relevant.

- He is known to be frequently late for meetings after scrambling to get documents prepared at the last minute.
- She sometimes forgets to record meetings on her calendar or to review the calendar altogether. She sometimes misses appointments or meetings because reminders are not centralized but rather found in a variety of places: in meeting notes, on sticky notes, on her calendar, in her PDA, and elsewhere.
- His computer desktop is cluttered with various documents, some of which are current important documents and others of which are old and no longer relevant.
- Computer files are being bounced between her office computer, laptop, and home computer, and multiple copies of the same document exist on multiple computers and USB drives. She is often unclear as to which copy is the latest.
- His e-mail inbox contains thousands of messages, many of which are more than 12 months old.
- She wastes many hours each week searching for lost documents (hardcopy as well as electronic), and she often has to call or e-mail others to help retrieve lost documents.

Has this list touched a sensitive area of your conscience? Don't worry. The organizational skills of virtually all department chairs I know have some room for improvement. The good news, however, is that being disorganized is not a chronic disease. Compared to other challenges that department chairs face, the goal of becoming organized is not difficult to achieve. It will require an upfront investment of time, but that investment will pay back many times later.

Organizing Your Office

Many faculty members, senior professors in particular, mistakenly believe that a messy office is a symbol of being busy and productive. They fear that a clean desk could be perceived as an indication that they do not have enough to do. They use this false image as an excuse for not getting organized, being late or absent at meetings, and being the last person to get important paperwork completed, and they often waste other people's time by asking for help in retrieving lost documents and files. The truth is that having a messy desk only symbolizes being disorganized, and there is nothing attractive about that. Cleaning up a messy office can be a major undertaking, certainly not a project suitable for a regular workday with lots of interruptions. The following three-day organizing process may be best implemented by allocating a series of not necessarily consecutive Saturdays or a few days during a semester break to get this done.

Day 1

Start day 1 at the office superstore. Get one or more document organizers (see Figure 5.1), and label the shelves, cubbyholes, or folders as follows:

  Inbox (incoming mail and new items to be reviewed)

  Outbox (should be emptied daily by secretary or assistant)

Figure 5.1 Commonly Used Document Organizers

Action Items: High Priority

Action Items: Low Priority

Filing: Personnel Matters (should be emptied daily by secretary or assistant)

Filing: Chair's Office (for you to file)

Filing: Department Office/Archive (should be emptied daily by secretary or assistant)

Upcoming Meetings (for your own use)

Classroom Observations (for use in faculty evaluations)

If you are teaching classes, you should also have a designated space where you keep lecture notes, folders for incoming home-work and assignments, and other class materials.

Now clear your desk, using the newly labeled organizers as well as a large wastebasket or recycling bin. Use the 4D principle (Crandell, 2005):

Do: Handle the item now if you can do it in five minutes or less.

Delegate: Label the item and put it in your outbox.

Defer: File the item as an action item. (If this is reference material not needed at the moment, put it on the "Filing: Chair's Office" shelf.)

Delete: If none of the above applies, use the wastebasket or recycling bin.

Once you have cleaned off your desk, only the following items should remain on it:

- Your telephone
- A cup for your pens
- Note pads and sticky notepads
- A business card holder

- A framed picture or two of your loved ones
- Documents that you are working on right now

You may choose to have a few other items on your desk, such as a desk lamp, office tools or supplies you use frequently, or display items that you are particularly proud of, but make sure you have plenty of space to spread out documents that you are currently working on. Clear the desk at the end of each day. Also clear your bulletin board frequently. You may want to post a copy of your colleagues' office hours, the current course schedule, and other current documents, but do not clutter it with too many historical display items. If there is a document you are particularly proud of, consider framing it and hanging it on your wall instead.

Day 2

On day 2 you should go through all of your shelves (or folders). Sort books and reports appropriately by topic. Keep books for your classes separate from books for your research. Place reference books on one shelf, university reports and catalogs on another. Get rid of textbooks for which you have a newer edition or books that you can't think of a need for. Unless your institution has a different policy or practice for disposing of textbooks and books purchased by university funds or provided to you by the publisher, make these available for students to pick up, and recycle those that have not been picked up within, say, a week. Avoid giving away textbooks that are labeled "Instructor's Edition" or "Instructor's Manual," as they generally contain answers to the questions in the textbook, which may pose a problem for other instructors. Also, if you have evaluation copies of textbooks in their current editions but you don't intend to use them, return these to the publisher. Publishers will pay the return shipping cost, and you will help your students by keeping textbook prices lower by doing so. Let your secretary or assistant handle the process of packaging and returning these books. If there are books that you for some reason cannot part with right now but you don't need in the foreseeable future, you may want to fill up a box and put it in your department storage room, labeled with your name, the content, and today's date.

Day 3

Day 3 of your organizing project involves going through your filing cabinets. This could take you more or less than one day, depending on how deep you want to dig into old file folders. Like your shelves, your files should be organized by topic. Keep files related to your classes separate from files related to professional and scholarly activities, and keep files for committees you are serving on as a faculty member separate from files related to your functions as a department chair. This will make it easier to transfer that portion of your file system to the next department chair (this is especially important if you are serving in a rotating chair position). Keep files in alphabetical order within each of the separate categories of your filing system.

As when sorting your books, get rid of files that you can no longer think of any use for, or pack a box for a storage archive if you feel a need to keep any files that will not be needed in the near future. For files that you are getting rid of, you will need to consider what to recycle and what to shred.

Organizing Your Department Filing System

If you have been fortunate, as I was, as a new chair you inherited a logically organized department filing system and an organized secretary or office assistant capable of maintaining it. But whether your department filing system needs a complete overhaul or is in good working condition, it is advisable for you to take some time to become familiar with the filing system and take a critical look at its operating procedures. A department filing system may include the following categories:

- Personnel (including faculty, staff, and part-time employees)
- Student employees
- Undergraduate majors and minors
- Graduate students (applicants and current students, including graduate assistants, if applicable)
- Curriculum (paperwork for course and program changes, past and ongoing)
- Courses offered (syllabi and course objectives)
- Transfer courses (records of decisions regarding courses accepted from other institutions)
- Course schedules (past and current, including data on enrollment)
- Department meetings (agendas, minutes)
- Policies and procedures (departmental and institutional)
- Textbooks (current and past orders)
- Course and room scheduling
- Program review, accreditation, and audits (internal and external)
- Strategic planning (including mission statement and annual action plans)
- Faculty and staff recruitment (applicants for current job openings)
- Student recruitment (files for prospective students, recruitment materials)
- Advertising and promotions (masters of brochures, fliers, and other documents)
- Awards and scholarships (for students, staff, and faculty)
- Directories (internal and external contact info)

- Computer software and hardware (disks, licenses, operating manuals)
- Access control (records of keys and IDs issued)
- Budgets
- Grants and contracts
- Institutional subscriptions and memberships

This list is by no means exhaustive, and some files may not be applicable to some departments. However, in creating files, I recommend not including generic files such as "Correspondence" or "Memos." Such files make filing easy but retrieving and maintaining files very difficult. Instead, correspondence should be stored in files appropriate to the content; for example, correspondence with a student should be filed in the student's advising file.

Like an old car, a department filing system needs periodic maintenance and service to keep it running smoothly. At least a couple of times a year (perhaps every semester), your filing system should be serviced by your staff by removing obsolete files, such as personnel files for faculty no longer employed and advising files for students who have graduated. Although this is a responsibility typically delegated to your staff, you may want to discuss with your staff some general rules for the maintenance of your department filing system. This may involve establishing practices that define what to keep (and for how long) and what to dispose of. Because this varies from institution to institution, I encourage you to schedule an appointment with your institution's legal adviser or someone from your human resource office to go over institutional policies on this matter. You may want to coordinate this effort with your dean's office, as other chairs in your college or school may have similar questions. The files of most concern are internal personnel files, candidate files for faculty searches, and financial exhibits such as receipts for travel and other expenses. There are certain files that you are required to keep, just as there are files that you are not allowed to keep. For example, I learned several years into my tenure as department chair that our university requires that past performance evaluations for classified employees be kept only in the office of human resources and that individual departments are not allowed to maintain copies of such evaluations that are more than one year old. Also, many state institutions are subject to open records laws. In the event that you are asked to provide access to files maintained in your office, it is very important that you know what to keep and what not to keep.

The security and privacy of your filing system are other major concerns. Files containing sensitive information, including personnel files, should be kept in a secure location, with access restricted to individuals with a need to know and to staff trusted to maintain the filing system. Why do I mention security and privacy in a book on time management? To illustrate the connection, imagine the consequences of a major breach of security in your department such as the theft of student and faculty Social Security numbers due to negligence on your part. The time involved in dealing with a significant breach of security (not to mention the financial impacts) would exceed by far the time required to implement simple precautions to protect the sensitive information for which you are responsible.

Organizing Your Computer

Today, the computer has become a focal point of everything we do as professionals. The number of documents we handle electronically now far exceeds the number we handle as hardcopies. Keeping your computer's filing system organized is at least as important as keeping your hardcopy filing system organized. The last time I checked, my office (laptop) computer contained approximately 30,000 documents and my home computer 55,000 documents. These numbers represent only the number of files located in the documents folders and do not include program or system files. Nearly all of these files are documents that I have created or downloaded at some point and include memos, correspondence, and course materials, as well as, for my home computer, music, pictures, and video files. If you have allowed chaos to develop on your computer, you may have one or more of the following problems:

- Multiple copies of the same document exist in various folders on your computer.
- Multiple copies of the same document exist on different computers and external media, including CDs, USB drives, and external hard disks.
- You have trouble locating the latest version of a given document.
- A large number of documents of various types exist on the desktop and in the root of the documents folder.

In extreme cases, getting your computer organized can be a much more time-consuming task than getting your physical office organized. To begin with, I recommend that you create a "data management plan." In this plan you will identify (in the form of a diagram) all of the various devices you use and all your portable media and indicate how they interact. Figure 5.2 illustrates such a network of devices. The arrows indicate the primary direction of data transfer, so the device from which the arrow originates is the device that generally has the most current version of a file when multiple copies exist. For example, a digital camera generates data (pictures) that are then transferred to a computer. An external hard disk primarily receives data to be stored in the form of backup files transferred to an archival folder, except when occasionally data are retrieved from a backup or archival copy. A mobile communication or Internet device (such as a BlackBerry) synchronizes with another computer, such that both devices are intended to host the most current version of the same files (primarily e-mail messages).

Figure 5.2 Managing Data Through the Use of Multiple Computing and Storage Devices

Once you have a data management plan defined, you can begin the time-consuming process of transferring files to their proper host or home folders. When merging files from several computers and portable media, there are tools available that delete outdated files and keep only the latest version of a document (or last version worked on). Because this falls outside the scope of this book, you are encouraged to consult with a computer wizard as you attempt to organize your electronic files in accordance with your data management plan. Following your data management plan also requires some discipline. When a file is temporarily removed from its host computer to be worked on with a different computer—for example, through a USB storage device—the folder that hosts the file temporarily being "checked out" needs to be clearly identified with a qualifier such as "Working On," "Revising," or "Draft." Upon return to the host computer, the file on the portable device should be transferred and deleted to avoid version conflict. Backup needs to be performed at regular intervals—daily, weekly, or monthly, depending on the level of protection desired. Software is available that automates the backup procedure.

We noted earlier the issue of keeping your physical files secure by restricting access to individuals with a "need to know" and preventing unauthorized access. It is at least equally important to keep your electronic data secure. Data security is provided through the use of user names and passwords; however, such protection is only as good as your management of your supposedly secret user names and passwords. Because of the large number of computer accounts that the average person controls nowadays (computer access, multiple e-mail accounts, student information systems, financial records, online shopping accounts, and so on), it is not uncommon for one person to have dozens of user names and passwords to manage. Because the typical person is not capable of memorizing so many user names and passwords, people often resort to two common practices that may have catastrophic consequences should a breach of security occur. One is to use the same user name and password for all accounts. Consequently, a person who gains unauthorized access to one of your accounts will have gained access to all of your accounts. The other common practice is to write down the various user names and passwords on a piece of paper that is kept in a drawer in the office. Not only is there a significant risk that you may lose that piece of paper, but there is an even greater risk that someone with access to your office will find this information. An alternative to these practices is to write down all of your user names and corresponding passwords in a text document or spreadsheet, but rather than printing out the list and storing it in your drawer, save this file in an encrypted partition of your computer's hard drive. There are several free encryption tools available, such as TrueCrypt (www.truecrypt.com). You can use this secure partition to store other documents of a sensitive nature. This procedure will require you to memorize only two sets of user names and passwords, one for the computer itself and one to access the encrypted partition. Because you will use these credentials frequently, they are not easily forgotten.

The final question to consider is, How portable are your data? Are you using proper caution in handling sensitive, confidential data—for example, when carrying such data on USB drives or mobile computing devices? What would happen in the event of loss or theft of your portable device or laptop? I discuss this question in more detail in my article "Technology Trends in Mobile Communication" (Hansen, 2009a). Seeing that the technology described is this article will continue to evolve, you should contact your local information technology experts for an overview of the latest technology available for your use in keeping your data portable, private, and secure.

Organizing Your E-Mail

When I mentioned that my work computer contains 30,000 documents, that number does not accurately account for the number of e-mail messages stored on the computer because many of them are consolidated into a single file. As a department chair, I received approximately one thousand e-mail messages each month, not including spam messages that were filtered out or automatically deleted. As with your physical office and computer, organizing your e-mail folders can be a time-consuming task if not done on a regular basis. Although sorting your messages into appropriate folders, just as you sort the documents in your filing cabinets, and deleting messages no longer needed would have some benefits, I personally do not recommend this approach for the purpose of organizing e-mail. There are two main reasons for this. First of all, unlike your physical space, computer storage space is cheap. Adding physical space to your office would be costly, if not impossible. But you can double or even increase by tenfold the hard disk space on your computer at a relatively nominal cost. Archiving computer files is very cheap (compared to the value of your time) and requires virtually no physical space. Usually it makes more sense to keep (and possibly archive) files rather than using your time to decide what to keep and what to delete.

Second, unlike your physical files, e-mail messages are easily "searchable." Even if you have 10,000 messages on your computer, in a matter of seconds you will be able to find the message you are looking for by searching for a particular sender, recipient, or keyword in the subject header or body of the message.

I am not advocating that you keep 10,000 messages in your inbox, but contrary to the advice of some time management experts, I don't have a problem with having a large number of messages stored in my inbox as long as they are all *recent* messages. Here is a practice that has worked well for me:

1. When reviewing incoming messages, use the 4D principle you use for sorting your physical files:

    Do: Reply and handle the matter if it can be done in five minutes or less.

    Delegate: Forward the message to the appropriate person, and record the item on your master task list (or set a reminder) if you need to keep track of the progress.

    Defer: Flag the message as a "to-do," and enter it on your master task list.

    Delete: Use the Delete key for spam and other messages you know for sure you will never need again. If in doubt, leave as "read" in your inbox.

2. Create folders for the types of messages that you need to refer to frequently without doing a search. That may include a folder for "Personnel Matters," one for each special project you are working on, and so on. Make it a

habit to drag e-mails into the appropriate folder upon receipt, or take some time at the end of the day or week to sort the latest e-mail into folders.

3. Archive e-mail periodically. When e-mail is archived, it is removed from your regular workspace, including the e-mail server, but it can still be retrieved with just a few clicks. Archive e-mail at the end of each academic term. Keep archives of e-mails from the last few terms on your work computer so that you can still easily access those messages (unless you are working on a device that can only access the mail server). Move e-mail archives that are more than a year old from your work computer to an external hard drive. You may choose to permanently delete messages beyond a certain age, but unless storage space becomes an issue, you don't need to worry about that.

Organizing Your Calendar

In Chapters Two and Four we discussed the importance of scheduling your priorities. The calendar is the blueprint of your workweek. Although some executives still successfully use a paper calendar, I strongly recommend the use of an electronic networked (shared) calendar. The main disadvantage of the old-fashioned paper calendar is that there is only one copy available to work on and hence only one person can handle your calendar at any given time. If you put your assistant in charge of managing your calendar, you are at a disadvantage, never knowing when your next appointment is. When you are in a meeting and you need to schedule a time to continue the discussion, this can be an impediment. With a shared calendar, you can control other people's ability to view and schedule appointments on your calendar. For those with "view only" access, you can also control how much detail they see; for example, you may want to keep certain appointments private, showing up as "busy" or "out of the office." You can (and should) allow your assistant to schedule appointments, but you also have the ability to schedule appointments yourself if you so choose. The availability of inexpensive handheld devices allows you to easily bring your current calendar with you to meetings.

The use of a shared calendar system is most effective when everyone you work with uses the same system. If you don't, you are likely to receive e-mails that start out something like this: "I am trying to set up a meeting to discuss. . . . Can you please let me know which times you are available to meet next week?" Once everyone has replied, you may find that there is no specific time that everyone can commit to, and so the whole process starts over again, trying to find a convenient time the following week. This process of scheduling meetings wastes a lot of valuable time that everyone could have used for more important tasks. As the leader of your department, it is your responsibility to promote wide adoption of the calendar system you are using. With a common system, you or your assistant can quickly set up a meeting, not only being able to see instantly who is available and when. Your institution may even have a calendar system that allows you to book a conference room through the same system.

Overcoming Procrastination

Procrastination (Fiore, 2006) is often referred to as the "thief of time" or even the "thief of life" (Dobbins and Pettman, 1998). You are procrastinating when you are "putting things off until you are too late or forced to work quickly to meet a deadline, and the quality of your results suffer" (Bond, 1991). Some tasks often take longer to complete than anticipated, and waiting only compounds the problems you are ignoring. But why do I mention this in a chapter that deals with getting organized? Because procrastination and personal disorganization are often linked. Procrastinators put off getting things organized often because the situation has gotten to a point where it is too overwhelming and unpleasant to deal with. Disorganized people often put off getting started on a major project because they have not yet organized all the required materials and personnel needed to get the project started. You may hear them say "as soon as I get things organized, we will get started."

But is it always a bad thing to put things off? Only if you are indeed procrastinating. Here are a few things to consider in determining whether you are procrastinating or simply postponing things that really should be postponed:

- Are you deferring tasks that are not important because other tasks take a higher priority?
- Do you have all of the information necessary to act now, or should you wait until you do?
- Is it possible that if you wait, the problem you are facing may disappear or become easier to solve?
- Do you need time to carefully consider your options or to calm down before you act?

If you answered yes to any of these questions, procrastination is not the problem. But procrastination is still a problem for many people and a tough habit to break. The best way to overcome the habit is to notice when you are procrastinating (using the four questions to guide you) and then keep reminding yourself that you are doing so. Break larger "procrastination-prone" tasks into smaller ones on your to-do list, and make a goal to complete at least one of these each week (or each day, depending on how ambitious you are).

Questions to Consider and Practical Tips

- Schedule one or more "cleanup" blocks, preferably during a weekend, semester break, or other time when you can work without interruptions (this is a "big rock" activity). Pick a single theme for each cleanup, such as "organize shelves," "organize filing system," or "organize e-mail."

- If you are transferring computer files between two or more computers, make it a priority to create a data management plan. Define which types of files are hosted on each computer, and make a plan for checking out and synchronizing files shared between computers.

- Make a plan, or review your current plan, for backing up of your computer files. Are backups scheduled frequently enough so that a fatal crash of your computer occurring at the worst possible time would not cause you to lose significant work that cannot easily be recovered? Is there a possibility of a single-point failure, such as your building burning down to the ground with both your computer and all backup copies? If so, what can you do to eliminate the possibility of a single-point failure?

- How secure are your computer and paper files? In the worst-case scenario, such as your computer being stolen or your building broken into, do you have sensitive information that can easily be retrieved by a third party? If so, how can you improve the security of your files? Keep in mind that any breach of security can cost you both time and money.

Part Two

WORKING WITH PEOPLE

6

YOU CAN'T DO IT ALL

Delegating

> Trust men and they will be true to you; treat
> them greatly, and they will show themselves
> great.
>
> —*Ralph Waldo Emerson*

As a faculty member, I served several years on the rules committee of our faculty organization. Various issues were brought before
this committee and would often be debated intensely by its
members before one particular seasoned member of the committee would interrupt by saying something like "May I remind us
that the charge of this committee is to direct issues to the appropriate committee or council to be acted on. It is not the charge
of this committee to act on the issue itself."

The role of the department chair in many ways is similar to
that of the rules committee. Almost every issue to be acted on
by a department is brought to the department chair, but it is not
the chair's job to act on every issue alone. Rather, it is the chair's
responsibility to route each particular issue to the appropriate
person or committee—in other words, to "direct the traffic." The
single largest time management issue of most new department
chairs is that they do not have a good sense of what issues to
handle themselves and what issues to defer or delegate to someone
else. There are two types of issues that we need to be concerned
about: decisions and tasks.

Delegating and Referring Decisions

Many of the decisions a department chair must make are related to budgets. Routine budget decisions regarding faculty travel and minor purchases for which a budget has been set aside or a policy exists should be made by the chair with minimal consultation with others except (if necessary) the staff person in charge of maintaining the department budget. When requests for funds exceed available funds, the chair may want to consult a planning committee or even the department as a whole in establishing priorities of what gets funded. The larger the funds being requested and the larger the gap between what is being requested and what is available, the greater the need for the chair to consult others before a decision is made. Budget decisions should not be made simply on the basis of equality. Rather decisions should be based on established goals and objectives for the department as discussed in Chapter Two. Budget decisions should be *rational* rather than *political* (Gmelch and Miskin, 2004). Such decisions usually involve subjective judgment and may cause negative reactions in the department if there is a perception that the chair is making too many unilateral decisions without consulting faculty. But what does this have to do with time management? This is in fact a major time issue, and one for which the best practices appear to be somewhat counterintuitive. Delegating decisions to others initially takes *more* time than simply making the decision alone. But the time it consumes later having to deal with conflicts that may result from the chair's making decisions without consulting others usually far exceeds the extra time it takes to consult. Which decisions can be made by the chair alone and which should be referred to others vary greatly from department to department. A seasoned chair who has developed solid trust with his or her colleagues will be expected to make more decisions alone than a new chair. The following list provides some guidelines based on my own experience.

Decisions Made by the Chair Without Further Consultation

- Approval of professional travel within established policies and available budget
- Approval of minor purchases for which funding is available
- Minor changes to the course schedule not significantly affecting faculty
- Response to requests from students (for example, related to course substitutions or equivalencies) for which an existing policy guides the decision
- Approval of leave requests and time sheets for staff (and faculty, if applicable)
- Hiring of part-time faculty
- Assignment of office space
- Approval of routine curriculum changes (such as adjustments of program requirements necessary due to changes in other departments)
- Nomination of faculty for awards

Decisions Requiring Prior Consultation of Individual Faculty or a Committee

- Approval of professional travel in excess of the available budget
- Approval of major purchases that require prioritization with other requests
- Response to requests from students that involve a major deviation from existing policy
- Planning the course schedule and issues related to workload (consulting is necessary with every faculty member involved)

- Personnel actions (usually university policy requires a recommendation from a personnel committee in addition to the recommendation from the chair)
- Approval of minor curriculum changes (may be handled by the appropriate curriculum committee)

Decisions Made by the Department as a Whole

- Hiring of faculty and staff (based on recommendations from a search committee)
- Strategic planning and development of long-range goals and action plans
- Creation of new policy or revision of existing policy
- Selection or nomination of students for awards and scholarships
- Approval of major curriculum changes, such as new courses or programs

Delegating Tasks to Faculty

In principle, everything can be delegated. Department chairs *are* faculty members and should be careful about thinking of themselves as indispensable or superior to their faculty colleagues. In particular, a chair should never fall into the trap of thinking that there are certain tasks that only he or she is capable of doing. If you as department chair are working many more hours than your faculty colleagues, that may be an indication that you are not delegating enough. Following is a list of tasks that may be delegated to faculty rather than being handled by the chair; keep in mind that this may vary from department to department.

- Curriculum development, including the development of new courses and programs
- Drafting a policy for department discussion
- Mentoring new faculty and graduate students

- Conducting faculty searches
- Student recruitment and outreach efforts (the chair should not be the only faculty member attending open houses or networking with local high schools and community colleges)

When delegating tasks to faculty, focus on desired outcomes rather than on methods. Faculty are professionals like you; they are not your hired help. When delegating a task to a faculty member (on your own behalf or as a committee chair), be sure to discuss the following matters:

- Authority: Who is responsible for the final decision if the task involves one?
- Resources: What budget or staff resources are available to support this task?
- Time line: When is this due?
- Status reporting needed: What milestones, if any, will be reported on along the way?
- Accountability: What are the incentives for doing this and the consequences for not doing it?

Faculty members are generally very good at saying no. Everyone understands their freedom to choose, and delegating a matter does not happen just by forwarding the issue to a faculty member. Delegation in academia usually happens through the process of negotiating.

Delegation from Faculty to Chair

In industry, tasks are created at a high level and delegated downward toward the lowest level of the organization at which the required expertise exists. Many classical time management books strongly warn about "upward delegation": subordinates' assigning their supervisors work to do. But in academia, delegation is a two-way street, and some of the upward delegation that the time management literature warns about is in fact a common and healthy practice. The faculty do not just work for the department chair; the chair also works for the faculty. Some tasks are delegated from chair to faculty, and other tasks are delegated in the other direction. This is true also in the relationship between chairs and higher-level academic administrators. Once one of our vice-provosts attended our college chairs' meeting. As he left the meeting, he noted, "I see that I am leaving with a longer list of things to do than the one I came here with."

Some people may disagree with my using the terminology "upward delegation," but what I am referring to here are simply issues that originate with the faculty and are passed on to the chair "to look into." As mentioned earlier, there really are no issues that only a department chair can handle, but there are some issues that are *best* handled by the chair, mainly those that require representation of the highest level of authority in the department. Here is an example of a situation that may involve delegating a task from faculty to the chair.

Example

The academic schedule at University X includes a 10-week-long quarter followed by a finals week. All regularly scheduled courses have assigned time slots for their finals, and university policy prohibits instructors from scheduling their finals at other times. Nevertheless, many instructors have adopted the practice of scheduling early finals during the last week of classes and giving students finals week off. In fact, many departments are known for notoriously violating the university's final exam policy. In the math department, however, there is usually so much material to cover that instructors would not want to give students early finals even if they had the option to do so. This brings up a series of issues because students in math classes often end up skipping class during the last week because of conflicts with finals scheduled by other classes requiring their attention. Furthermore, students complain about having to take math finals during finals week, indicating that "other classes don't make us stay another week."

The issue just described is clearly one that individual faculty would have a hard time dealing with on their own and naturally a matter that they would ask the chair to do something about. In this case, a chair is in a much better position to discuss the concern with chairs from the "offending" departments and if necessary bring the issue to the dean or a higher-level administrator. Other issues that may justify faculty delegating a matter to their chair include the following:

- Any issue requiring negotiations with another department or a higher-level administrator and for which authority is a concern (this includes most budget requests)
- Issues with students or faculty that involve allegations of discrimination or harassment
- Issues with students exhibiting disruptive behavior in class
- Suspicions of alcohol or drug abuse on campus (among students or faculty)
- Dealing with an upset parent
- Issues requiring someone to speak with news media
- Issues of "bad publicity" on or off campus

A department chair must exercise good judgment in deciding which issues to accept responsibility for and which ones to refer to someone else. Often a chair will get requests from faculty to provide a letter in support of something (say, a grant proposal) or a letter expressing concern about something. But being willing to represent the department or one or more faculty on some matter does not necessarily mean that the chair has to do all the work involved. For example, cases that involve sending a letter supporting or expressing concern about a matter could be initiated by asking a faculty member to prepare a draft of a letter and e-mail it to you for editing and signature.

Delegating Tasks to Staff

Much of the classic time management literature has made the suggestion that a manager or executive is only as good as his or her staff. The same holds true for department chairs. Good secretaries and office assistants are treasures that are hard to find and when found should be treated as gold. As a department chair, I was fortunate to have very competent staff, including a highly experienced secretary who had been with the university for nearly two decades. She made my job so much more manageable and enjoyable, and I used every opportunity I could get to let her know how valuable she was to me and how much I appreciated her loyalty to the department. On the opposite end of the scale, I have also witnessed examples of other departments with a "poisonous" secretary, someone who appears to be doing everything possible to sabotage what the department chair does. If a staff person (or faculty member for that matter) wants to make your life miserable, it's not hard to do. Staff, good or bad, can make or break a department chair. If you have been blessed with dedicated and competent staff, treat them well and express your gratitude to them every day. If you have staff that in spite of every effort you have made are not able or willing to improve, you must face the battle of getting rid of them. Firing a staff member is generally a difficult and time-consuming process that will involve the support of both your dean and your faculty colleagues. If replacing a secretary or staff person who is not cooperating is not a battle you wish to engage in, consider moving on to other career opportunities. Being a department chair without good staff is just not a realistic option.

Treating staff well is not just a matter of thanking them and nominating them for awards. They must be empowered and inspired to seek their highest potential and feel that they make a valuable contribution to your department and institution. As with faculty, delegate tasks with stewardship. Focus on results rather than on methods, and clarify authority, resources, time line, milestones, and accountability. In some cases, breaking a larger project into smaller tasks may be helpful; in other cases, it is better to let the staff member establish the tasks. Other recommendations in working with staff include the following:

Be a Resource. I recommend that you frequently ask your staff for suggestions on things that could make their job more effective. Don't just assume that they will ask if there is something they need. If a new piece of equipment, new furniture, or a training seminar is the answer, make it a priority to find the funding to provide it. Such investments usually pay off many times.

Hire Student Employees. Students can bring substantial value to a department. Students offer inexpensive assistance, and they are usually eager for the opportunity to gain professional experience while making money to support their studies. But be sure to delegate the responsibility of hiring and supervising your student employees to a trusted member of your staff. Student employees will require more supervision than your staff, but like staff, student employees should be gradually delegated more and more tasks with stewardship. You may even be able to hire students who possess talent that can be valuable to the department beyond just making photocopies and running errands. For example, a computer science major may be able to help maintain your department's Web site and perform basic maintenance of your department's computers. An English or journalism major may be able to help proofread letters or reports for you.

Plan Ahead. Protect your staff's time in the same way that you want to protect your own. Secretaries do not like having stuff dumped in their lap at the last minute. Planning ahead for deadlines and major projects that need staff support will make their job much easier and more time-effective.

Be Flexible. Secretaries need their vacations and personal leave, and term breaks can be a difficult time for them to take time off. Be accommodating when they request leave, even if the timing is not convenient for you. There is almost never a good time for you to be without your key staff, so unless the request for leave is clearly unreasonable, you should give priority to accommodating your staff's needs for leave.

Delegating Acting Chair Responsibilities

On occasions when the department chair will be on vacation or attending a conference, it may be necessary to appoint an acting chair to perform all of the functions of the department chair in his or her absence. Handing over signing authority to someone else requires substantial thought. Who in your department has developed the necessary trust with you and the department and has the right qualifications to be suitable for this very demanding assignment? There are three types of people that naturally come to mind: an associate chair, a former chair, and a potential future chair.

If your department is large enough to have an associate chair, that would be someone you already have a trusted relationship with and typically a person who already knows (or should know) the operating procedures around your office. Also, particularly in departments that use a rotating department chairmanship, it is likely that there are one or more former chairs among the faculty. There may even be some that are emeritus faculty who are still active in the department and willing to step in on your behalf for a few days. Being a former chair, however, does not make everyone a prime candidate for this assignment. You would want to choose someone who is trusted not just by you but by the department in general. Only someone who left the chair position in good standing should be considered.

A third possibility is a faculty member in your department that you would support as a potential replacement for yourself if and when you step down. In fact, that might be the best choice of all because appointing a prospective future chair as acting chair gives the person an opportunity to learn about your job and gradually become socialized into the position.

Regardless of which of the three types you choose, you will need to have your candidate for this assignment identified soon after you take on the chair position. Once you have selected a person who is able and willing to serve as acting chair when called for, discuss your choice with your dean. That way, should the dean have any objections to your choice, it can be discussed before the actual situation arises, and also the dean will know whom to appoint in the unfortunate event that illness or an accident prevents you from making the temporary appointment yourself. Whenever possible, you should select the same person each time you are away.

Once you have made the choice, take advantage of each opportunity to try out the person by appointing him or her to serve even when you go on a short business trip for a day or two. That way, you will have a better chance to work out any problems before you have this person fill in for you for a longer period. Each time a situation that calls for the assignment of an acting chair arises, send a memo announcing your intentions to your dean at least a couple of days in advance, with copies to all of your faculty and staff. Also post a copy of the memo on your door to redirect unannounced visitors appropriately. That note might read as follows:

> I will be out of the office on _____ attending the _____, during which time Dr. _____ has agreed to serve as acting chair. Dr. _____ is authorized to sign for and act on behalf of the department on all matters ordinarily handled by the chair until my return. For matters needing my personal attention, I can be reached on my cell phone (please contact _____ for assistance).

Although you are appointing someone as the acting chair during your absence, it does not mean that this person will be performing all of the same duties that you normally would during the same period. Remember that this person is doing this on top of his or her regular duties, including a full teaching load. You should make every possible attempt to make the job of your acting chair as easy as possible. First, attempt to reschedule any important meetings you were scheduled to attend during your absence. For meetings you cannot reschedule, be sure to let others involved know that you will have someone attend on your behalf. Check with your secretary to see if there are any critical items, such as a schedule proof, that needs to be signed before you leave or during your absence. If anything has to be signed while you are gone, discuss these items with your acting chair so that the responsibilities involved are clear. Discuss any foreseeable situations in which you would want to be consulted before an acting chair signs off, and unless you are on vacation, let your signee as well as your secretary know your schedule and when you will be able to check your voice and e-mail messages.

Following a well-thought-out process when appointing an acting chair during your absence is crucial to time management. Having established expectations and responsibilities and discussed various "what if" scenarios saves time for everyone involved, and you will be able to rest easy in your hotel room knowing that you have left the department in good hands and that you will not face a time-consuming mess to clean up when you get home.

Finally, if you are serving as department chair in a term of indefinite length (at the pleasure of your dean) or if you have been serving multiple elected terms, you should consider planning a sabbatical to renew your energy and remain current in your profession. When appointing an acting chair for an entire academic term or beyond, you should not plan to remain in contact with the daily operation of the department in the same way as when you leave for vacation or a conference. In this case, you will be fully handing over the reins to someone else, and the person you choose should be given at least the same release time from teaching as you normally enjoy. If possible, plan to spend your sabbatical where you cannot easily be reached. If you end up being contacted every day by your secretary or the acting chair about how to handle one thing or another, it will greatly limit what you will accomplish during your sabbatical.

Questions to Consider and Practical Tips

- Do you consider yourself effective in delegating tasks to faculty and staff? If not, what are some of the factors that prevent you from delegating effectively, and how can some of these challenges be overcome without extra resources?

- Are there people among your faculty or staff that you know you can always count on when you delegate tasks to them even if they are already busy? Are there others who are always reluctant to take on tasks even though they don't seem all that busy? For the latter group, what would motivate them to accept more tasks that you wish to delegate to them?

7

TAKING CHARGE

Making Meetings Work

A committee is a group that keeps minutes and
wastes hours.

—*London Tit-Bits*

Some data suggest that department chairs spend about 50 percent
of their time in scheduled meetings (Gmelch and Miskin, 2004),
and faculty members spend a significant portion of their time in
department meetings, committee meetings, university task force
and council meetings, and the like. A department chair has a
strong influence on how much time he or she will spend in meetings and what is accomplished during these meetings.

In this chapter I will limit the discussion to the practice of
conducting regular faculty meetings (involving all department
faculty), but virtually all the same principles apply to the conduct
of smaller group (committee) meetings. Based on my conversations with many academics in a variety of institutions and disci-
plines, I have concluded that most academic departments need
one or more of the following:

- Fewer and shorter meetings
- More effective use of time in meetings
- More and better interpersonal communication outside
  of meetings

A crucial point here is that we *need* interpersonal communication (that is, two-way communication) in order to do our jobs

effectively, but most meetings do not promote this type of communication either because the topics discussed are irrelevant for most of the participants or because most of the meeting time is spent on one-way communication, such as announcements and reports. Many meetings are merely an organized form of socializing where the agenda is used to initiate a drifting conversation of topics of interest to some members, mostly issues for which many have concerns but few have any influence over.

The focus of this chapter will be on principles and criteria that might be applied in order to make meetings more productive, reduce the need for meetings, and free up time for more important tasks.

The Cost of Meetings

It may be helpful to develop an idea of the cost of faculty meetings in time and money. Let's say you have twenty members of your faculty and that you hold meetings twice a month that each last two hours. Accounting for quarter or semester breaks, this amounts to approximately sixteen meetings a year, taking up a total of 640 hours, or four months of faculty time collectively. If you figure conservatively $50 per hour in average salary and benefits, the total cost of these meetings is $32,000 per year in faculty time alone (not counting cost of staff, meeting space, photocopies, coffee and cookies, and so on). Do the results produced at those meetings justify this cost? How many courses could have been taught or research articles supported for the same investment of time and money? The calculation I just did roughly reflects the situation of the department I was chairing, a department that has had a long tradition of holding faculty meetings twice a month. At the time I took over as chair, it would have been unwise to change the frequency of meetings. Reducing the number of faculty meetings would have been perceived as an attempt to keep faculty "out of the loop." However, several years later, after having established a high level of trust among the

faculty, I was able to reduce time spent in faculty meetings somewhat. Although meetings were still scheduled twice a month, I
would sometimes cancel a meeting if there were no substantive
items to act on, and meetings scheduled to last two hours were
often conducted in an hour or less.

When to Call a Meeting

A department meeting should be called only when there is a
need for the entire department to resolve one or more issues that
cannot be resolved by the chair alone or by a smaller group of
faculty. That includes issues that could be decided by one person
alone but are better decided based on the collective expertise of
the entire faculty. For example, a decision on which students
should be given graduation awards could certainly be made by a
department chair alone, but the collective group of faculty is in
a better position to make an informed decision, given their more
in-depth experience with each of the students in the classroom.
The decision to approve a faculty member's request for travel
funds, by contrast, is usually best made by the chair alone. The
chair knows (or should know) the balance of funds committed
to each faculty member and what allocations are possible and
equitable in consideration of the department budget. The collective faculty have no solid basis for making such decisions and
will instead base them on their personal feelings toward the
faculty members in question. In general, issues related to awards,
policymaking, and strategy are best made by the department,
while issues related to the daily operation of the department are
best made by the chair alone, perhaps in consultation with a
smaller executive or curriculum committee.

Agendas

Meetings should never be held without an agenda. An agenda
should contain items of business that require a decision most

appropriately made by more than one person. It is unfortunately very common that meetings are held simply because dates for them have been scheduled at regular intervals. Because in many cases the faculty members have either a direct or implied obligation to attend a meeting when called, this places all of the responsibility on the chair who is calling the meeting to make sure that the meeting is justified.

Agendas should generally be prepared and distributed at least a day before the meeting. This allows the participants to propose additions or amendments to the agenda and to prepare for the business items being handled. Agendas should be composed using the "big rocks" principle discussed in earlier chapters such that the items of highest priority are discussed early in the meeting and not accidentally overlooked in favor of less important business. It may be necessary to include some reports or announcements, but the person presiding over the meeting must carefully limit the time spent on those agenda items so that they do not use up time needed to finish important action items requiring a decision. Parkinson's Law applies to meetings just as it does to calendars. If a meeting is scheduled to last two hours, the time will tend to be completely filled by the items on the agenda. Another factor to consider is the order in which agenda items are to be handled. If guests or staff are attending only a portion of a meeting, their business should be covered first so as not to waste their time sitting through discussions of items of no relevance to them.

So, you may ask, what is the recommended frequency and length of faculty meetings? Unfortunately, there is no universal answer to that question. It depends on the size of the department and the culture of the decision-making process in that department. Some departments have strong leadership and the chair makes all or most decisions, and other departments are operated more like democracies where all major decisions are made collectively by the department as a whole. The greater the number of collectively made decisions, the more frequently the department will need to meet. There are, however, time management problems associated with either a too strong or a too weak form of department leadership. If the chair makes too many unilateral decisions, the faculty may feel that their voices are not being heard, and when decisions are made that have a negative effect on faculty, conflict and distrust are likely to develop. Conflict and lack of trust may end up being much more time-consuming than having the few extra meetings necessary to involve faculty in the decision process. However, if democracy is taken to the extreme, decisions may drag on forever, and faculty's time is wasted discussing business items for which they do not have enough information to make an informed decision. In other words, having too few meetings can be as much a time waster as having too many meetings. The challenge is to schedule just enough meetings so that faculty feel involved in the decision process and so that only business appropriate for joint decision making is handled in those meetings. As a department chair, you may want to establish a regular meeting schedule so that faculty can reserve the time on their calendar to attend, but convene the meetings only if sufficient business exists to make that meeting worthwhile.

If you are a new chair, it is important to learn about the culture of the decision process in the department and the faculty's expectations for involvement in decisions. Bialozor and Bialozor (2006) suggest that faculty members perceive four levels of involvement, from least to most:

1. "Just Do It" (no faculty involvement needed, the chair will handle this matter alone)
2. "Inform Me" (decision and implementation made by the chair and then reported to faculty)
3. "Consult Me" (faculty are consulted by the chair before any action by the chair is taken)
4. "Involve Me" (faculty are involved in the decision process and implementation)

Always ask yourself, At what level should the business item we are currently discussing be handled? Keep in mind that time is wasted when an item of business is handled at the wrong level.

Running a Meeting

When presiding over a faculty meeting, there are many things to consider in making the best use of the time available. Always begin the meeting on time. Don't wait for latecomers or attempt to recap the discussions for them as they show up. If it appears that you have a chronic problem with people showing up late (perhaps lacking a quorum), then you may need to have private conversations with the latecomers about their reasons for being tardy and the importance of having everyone ready to start the meeting on time. If the reason for many faculty being late is that they are coming out of class and have trouble getting to the meeting promptly (perhaps from the other side of campus), consider moving your starting time back 5 or 10 minutes.

A meeting is usually initiated with a brief review of the agenda and the minutes of the previous meeting. This is the only time that faculty may suggest changes to the agenda. If a member wishes to add a report or a new business item and there are no objections, simply add it to the agenda. Resist allowing a faculty member to bring up items that have already been debated and acted on.

A great time-saving idea is not to bring every routine matter up for a vote. Instead, use "implied consensus": for example, say, "Are there any changes to the minutes? (pause) Hearing no objections, I will consider the minutes approved by consensus."

Speaking of meeting minutes, it is my experience that writing up minutes can often be a drain on a secretary's time (especially if meetings are held frequently). Furthermore, if minutes are too long, most faculty do not bother reading them before they are approved. To reduce this type of time waster, consider coaching your secretary on keeping the minutes as brief as possible. Minutes should include a record of attendance, motions and their outcomes, and responsibilities assigned for action items. Summaries of discussions and reports should be kept to a minimum or not included at all. I once chaired a university council for which we had a secretary who could type faster than I could speak. In our council minutes, she would transcribe every sentence word for word and even include "sound effects" such as "(applause)" and "(laughter)." The minutes were often more than twenty pages long and would take me as long to proofread as the meeting itself took. Such a document format is appropriate in the performing arts or in courtrooms but not for academic department or committee meeting minutes.

When new and old business items are being debated, be sure to keep the discussion focused by not allowing discussions to drift or having a few people monopolize the discussion. Keep an eye on the clock, and watch out for people simply repeating points already made. Once all points in favor and opposed have been presented, it is time to move on. If this is a new business item, close the debate by saying, "I see this is an item of importance to many of us. I suggest that we table this motion and give it some further thought and discuss it among ourselves so that we can make a decision at our next meeting." If it is old business, say, "I think we have heard the statements both in favor and against the motion, so unless there are any additional points that we have not heard, let's go ahead and vote."

Sometimes a discussion can go on for quite a while before an actual motion is introduced. Although a chair cannot make motions, it is generally accepted that the chair will help state a motion that reflects the points being discussed. You may say, "May I entertain a motion that . . . ," which can be quickly adopted with a "so moved" response. Don't allow motions to be introduced if they are not coherent or have no real implication. Suppose you are discussing graduate student awards and from the discussion it appears that you are lacking a sufficient pool of qualified candidates. One of your faculty members says, "I move that we do not offer an outstanding graduate instructor award this year." Such a motion should always be dismissed as out of order because the outcome of the motion is exactly the same whether it passes or not; any time spent discussing or voting on a such motion would be wasted. In this situation, you may want to make a statement like "I am not hearing any suggestions for this award, so unless someone wants to make a nomination, I would like to move on to the next item."

Although, the main purpose of a meeting is to make decisions, it is natural and appropriate to use the opportunity to also make announcements and give reports. Such reports should be kept brief and be limited to issues of broad interest to the faculty. If the report cannot be summarized in five minutes or less, you may want to encourage the presenter to send out an e-mail with more detailed information and documentation to be perused by the members after the meeting.

Questions to Consider and Practical Tips

- Discuss the four levels of involvement discussed in this chapter with a few colleagues or you entire department, if appropriate. Which business items in your department are level 1 ("Just Do It"), and which are level 4 ("Involve Me")? Have you had a recent experience when time was wasted due to a business item being handled at the wrong level? What can you learn from this experience?

- How often does you department meet, and how much are these meetings costing your institution per year? Do the accomplishments of your meetings justify the cost of the meetings? Could the same results have been accomplished with fewer or shorter meetings?

- Faculty meetings should always be held in a positive, professional and pleasant atmosphere. It is important that the chair focus on running the meeting as a neutral moderator.

- Your role as chair is to control the debate and ensure that issues, not individuals, are attacked. Leave it to your colleagues to present arguments for or against the issue being debated. Keep the meeting moving, answer questions, and offer clarifications as needed, but avoid taking the floor to speak for or against an issue.

- A faculty meeting is not a social gathering, but that does not mean that you cannot provide an entertaining atmosphere and keep the conversation casual with brief (tasteful) quips or jokes at times.

- Hold a meeting only when there is a substantive agenda (items needing department action). If the agenda lists only reports and information items, cancel the meeting and have these materials distributed via e-mail by the appropriate parties.

- Be selective about who attends. Invite people to attend a meeting only if the items on the agenda affect them or people they supervise and if they have the ability to make an informed decision on items being voted on. If there are items that do not need to be discussed by the entire group of participants, refer those items to a committee or put them last on the agenda so that you can excuse the individuals who need not be involved in that portion of the meeting.

- Distribute the agenda in advance. This allows participants to come prepared and to gather all relevant information needed to make an informed decision.

- Come prepared. Anticipate what information will be relevant for the meeting, gather it in advance, and bring it to the meeting.

- Start meetings on time. Don't provide recaps of discussion points for latecomers.
- Stick to the agenda. Set a time limit for discussion of each item, and don't let discussions get off topic.
- Ask for 100 percent participation. A faculty meeting is not the appropriate venue for grading papers, surfing the Net, or checking e-mail or text messages on a laptop or smart phone.
- Finished means finished. Don't allow members to bring up items of business that have been previously finished. If a member insists, have him or her make a motion to revisit the previously finished item of business. This motion requires a second and a two-thirds majority to carry. Motions to revisit are not debatable.
- Go easy on the trees. Don't drown your faculty in handouts. Copy only the summary sheets, and have your secretary note down who needs full documentation after the meeting and then take responsibility for distributing those items. Whenever possible, use e-mail to distribute handouts and let faculty decide what they need to print. Bring a laptop to the meeting, and display documents that have not been distributed on a projector if the information is needed for the discussion.
- Refer an issue to the appropriate committee before it is brought to the entire department. Issues such as those related to curriculum should be discussed in a committee first. That way, the pros and cons have already been debated by a smaller and more specialized group, who can bring a seconded motion to the floor for a quick decision by the department.
- Give *Robert* a break. *Robert's Rules of Order* require that items of business are introduced first as "new business" and not acted on until the second meeting when discussed as "old business." In some cases, this can be a

waste of time. I suggest that your department adopt a policy that items introduced by a committee are acted on as "old business," thus allowing a more speedy decision. Occasionally, you may want to entertain a motion to "suspend the rules" to allow items of an urgent nature to be acted on at the meeting they are introduced.

8

THE ARTFUL LEADER

Working with Faculty and Students

> 80 percent of our time is spent with 20 percent
> of the people we work with.
> —Based on Pareto's 80/20 principle

It has often been noted that a college or university is only as strong as its faculty. Indeed, faculty are an institution's most valuable asset. Yet we also realize that a college or university cannot exist without students. Given the important role that faculty and students play at every academic institution and the amount of time a chair spends with each group of people, a book on time management for department chairs would not be complete without some discussion of how to manage time spent working with faculty and students.

Some academics view students as "customers"; however, this view leads to many contradictions in considering how to best serve our "customers." A former colleague once told me that "a university is the only business where the customers are happy if they get less than what they paid for." Department chairs must deal with a number of student concerns on a daily or weekly basis, including those that arise from disputes over grading and other student-faculty teaching issues. Such issues are more appropriately dealt with by considering students as the university's "product" rather than customers (Conway, 1996). It is the ultimate mission of every academic institution to recruit, retain, and graduate the highest-quality students, and concerns raised by students and parents must be addressed by looking for win-win solutions that address concerns while protecting our academic standards, or in other words, the quality of our "product."

Considering students as the product of the institution, the faculty may be considered the "engine" that produces this product. Two factors determine success in acquiring and developing a strong faculty: hiring the right faculty and empowering the faculty to achieve their maximum potential. These factors are in fact closely related. The potential of your faculty depends highly on the degree to which you have hired the right people to begin with, but your ability to hire the right faculty also depends on the quality of your current faculty. The process of hiring new faculty tends to take the form of either a vicious circle or a spiral of growth. The vicious circle results from the fact that poor faculty will tend to attract poor faculty, while excellent faculty will more easily attract excellent faculty. Turning a vicious circle into a spiral of growth poses a significant challenge.

Although some of the content of this chapter may seem peripheral to the subject of this book, the truth is that effective communication and interpersonal relations are essential to time management. The impact of these matters on time management is best observed in their absence. An environment of ineffective communication and poor relationships with faculty and students will likely lead to much wasted time and increased stress for any department chair.

Hiring Faculty

There are many excellent books on the subject of faculty hiring, so I will discuss the process of hiring only from a time management perspective. Any new hiring requires a substantial investment of both time and money. Some sources quoted by Hochel and Wilson (2007) cite a rule of thumb that the cost of a new hire is the equivalent of one year's salary for that person. Based on my own experience, I have estimated that the hiring of a new faculty member requires an investment of 500 to 1,000 hours of chair, faculty, and administrative and staff time from the early stages of justifying the position to the process of getting the new faculty member off to a great start. Adding the cost of interviewing expenses, startup funds, moving allowances, and other peripheral costs to the value of chair, faculty, and staff time committed, the total cost I arrive at is consistent with one year's salary. Making best use of chair and department time in the hiring process requires the use of many of the techniques discussed in the earlier chapters, including keeping things organized and delegating wisely. There are many time management issues to consider in each of the phases of the search, from justifying the position to welcoming and establishing a new faculty member. The details of the search process are beyond the scope of this book, but any chair should keep in mind that hiring faculty is not only a very expensive decision but also perhaps the most important product capability (PC) activity that a chair can engage in. Hiring right will save time in the long run; a failed search or a wrong hire could mean wasting 1,000 or more hours of department time.

I recently studied faculty hiring in my own department using data on faculty hired in the last two decades. Of the eighteen tenure-track faculty we hired, ten (56 percent) were still actively employed, six (33 percent) had resigned, and of the remaining two, one person was not retained and one died prematurely. Among those who resigned, the average length of service was 4.17 years, with none less than two or more than six. In contrast, the current faculty had accumulated an average of approximately 17 years of service. I don't know to what extent our data reflect national trends, but the numbers are alarming to me. Almost 40 percent of our recent hires ended up "not working out," meaning that they either left the university after a few years of service or did not perform to our expectations. Adding to that, we had several failed searches that resulted in no hiring for various reasons, which means that we probably wasted close to half of the time spent on searches, each costing us close to a year's salary.

Although factors beyond a department's control certainly do influence a faculty member's decision to leave (for example, a desire to relocate for family reasons), I also believe that there are many factors within a department's control. I personally believe that effective mentoring and empowerment are the most important ones.

Empowering Faculty

As emphasized earlier, a department's top priority should be to hire the best faculty to begin with. However, hiring the best faculty is of no value unless the department offers an environment that promotes faculty performance that maximizes the potential of each faculty member. This topic closely relates to department time, which is not managed effectively unless faculty are positively engaged and motivated to perform.

To this end, you must ask, What motivates faculty to perform at their best? Junior faculty may be motivated by the prospect of tenure and promotion, but that alone usually does not guarantee top performance. Not only will that motivation eventually disappear once promotion to the highest rank has been achieved, but also promotion and tenure requirements may cause junior faculty to simply focus on checking off achievements, focusing on what looks good on paper rather than what is best for the department. To promote top faculty performance, faculty must be empowered through intrinsic motivation, the kind of motivation that comes from within themselves, where the reward is based on the satisfaction of having a positive effect on other people's lives. Covey (2004b) refers to this kind of empowerment as finding your own "voice." Without intrinsic motivation, some faculty may continue to perform well, driven only by a desire to build their résumés and pursue jobs at other institutions, whereas other faculty will seek their satisfaction from outside the job and eventually fall into a state of being "retired on the job." Ideally, with intrinsic motivation, a senior faculty member who has reached the highest rank will feel the same motivation to perform as the newly hired junior faculty member. Faculty members are like plants that need consistent watering and nurturing for them to grow and blossom. From the chair's perspective, this is done through modeling of good work ethics, understanding and supporting the needs of the faculty members, recognizing and rewarding achievement, and aligning the faculty members' talent with the needs of the department.

It is important for a department chair to realize that every faculty member is different and therefore the efforts needed to motivate and empower faculty members will vary from one faculty to another. One of the most common reasons contributing to the failure of a department chair is to assume that all faculty are the same. I am not suggesting that a chair should give preferential treatment or "play favorites." The point I am making is that not everyone values the same things, nor does everyone have the same needs, talents, and weaknesses. What might be perceived as a fair share of resources by one person may be considered completely unfair by another. Ignoring the differences between faculty and using a political rather than rational process for distribution of resources and assignment of courses whereby everyone is treated the same and everyone gets the same share of everything will prevent any department from prospering and will promote mediocrity at best. Every department chair will be bounded by some politics with respect to the process of distributing resources, but the best chairs will use their influence to maximize the implementation of rational decisions over political decisions. Political decisions result in *equality*, but only rational decisions result in an *equitable* distribution of resources.

One tool that I highly recommend is what I call a faculty inventory analysis. This analysis involves looking at each of your faculty members and identifying his or her unique strengths and weaknesses, needs, preferences, and dislikes. Again, department policy may require some level of politics in distributing certain resources such as travel funds and assignment of teaching loads, but a chair often has a substantial amount of freedom to distribute resources and to assign courses, advising responsibilities, and department service activities. The primary goal is to maximize the use of each person's strengths while making their weaknesses irrelevant. Another goal is to balance the degree to which each person's needs are met and accommodating each person's prefer- ences and dislikes. To this end, diversity among faculty is extremely valuable. Among your faculty, you may have some people who love teaching early-morning classes and others who hate it. Some faculty members may be most competent at teach- ing graduate courses while others are happiest teaching lower level courses. Maximum performance and best use of faculty time are best achieved when faculty talent is aligned with department needs to the greatest extent possible. The more diversity you have among your faculty, the easier it will be for you to achieve this.

Dealing with Faculty Conflicts

If you have attended any conferences for department chairs, you may have noticed that they usually have at least one session or workshop titled something like "How to Deal with Difficult People," and those sessions usually draw packed crowds.

Again you may be asking, is this related to time management? Yes, it is. Its relevance is due to the fact that faculty conflicts can be a huge drain on a department chair's time, as well as a source of stress. Clearly, the best way to save time in this regard is to be proactive and prevent conflicts from arising in the first place or, when they do occur, to deal with them quickly to prevent small disagreements from turning into department-wide conflicts.

Conflict usually arises when two or more people see the same situation through different perspectives (Covey, 1989). Most conflicts are resolved through the application of strong commu- nication skills (Higgerson, 1996), in particular the art of empathic listening. Following are some examples of situations that may result in conflicts between faculty or between one or more faculty members and the department chair. For each of these situations, I have suggested ideas for time-saving solutions. Keep in mind, however, that every conflict is different and requires a unique solution that will depend on the circumstances and the people involved.

Situation 1: Professors Seek Independence

Most professors enjoy the role of being their "own boss." They are protective of the academic freedom to teach their courses as they see fit, to choose their scholarly activities, and to decide which service activities to engage in. Historically, professors have been able to come and go pretty much as they please and not be held accountable for how much time they spend on campus as long as they show up for required classes, office hours, and meetings. Recently, increased workloads and demands for accountability have threatened this freedom. Professors often have their own agendas, and whenever the question arises as to whether a faculty member's priorities are properly aligned with department or institution mission or goals, the potential for conflict soars.

Potential Solutions: Be sure to let the faculty member know that you respect and applaud the freedom associated with the faculty position. However, freedom and responsibility must coexist. A solution to the conflict must be found in the area where freedom and responsibility intersect. In searching for third alternatives, faculty must accept that institutional goals cannot be compromised, but a department chair and the administration must also accept that these goals must be achieved acknowledging the freedom of the faculty member to choose the methods and the schedule to accomplish them.

Situation 2: Professors Have Their Favorite Courses

Department chairs have to be sensitive to the needs of students in terms of courses needed for their major and university graduation requirements. The list of courses that are in high demand often differs from the list of courses faculty wish to teach. A potential for conflict often arises when the chair sees a necessity to reassign a professor from a low-enrollment specialized course for majors to a high-enrollment general education course.

Potential Solutions: Have a faculty committee (such as the curriculum committee) work out the first draft of the course schedule, but be sure to specify any constraints that reflect department and student needs and workload expectations. The chair should have final authority over the schedule, but it saves time and creates better morale if faculty can work out assignment conflicts on their own. Faculty may not always get their first choice met this way, but my experience is that faculty tend to be more satisfied with their teaching assignment if they feel that they got their "fair share" (of good and bad) and that their preferences are being taken into consideration by their colleagues and the chair.

Situation 3: Professors Come with Baggage

The academic institution offers much less mobility than the business professions. Because many departments have several faculty that have been around for generations, there is inevitably much baggage that is being carried around—old conflicts between faculty members, various personal likes and dislikes, and perhaps even some "good old boys" coalitions that have created biases toward certain people. When faculty coalitions consistently work against each other owing to personal issues rather than issues of real substance, both time and effectiveness are lost.

Potential Solutions: A department that finds itself deadlocked due to faculty conflicts and lack of collegiality may need to bring in outside help. Be sure to seek advice from your dean before considering bringing in someone from outside. Furthermore, with or without help from outside, the department chair can contribute to reducing hostility by being a role model for the rest of the department. This may involve taking a neutral position on issues that divide the department, focusing on creating and expanding common ground, and never speaking negatively about anyone not present.

Sometimes in the process of understanding a problem and working toward a solution, things can get ugly. One final piece of advice I would give for dealing with conflicts (with faculty, staff, or students) is to always *separate the person you are from the position you hold*. You may find yourself in a situation where you are being yelled at or called offensive names. Such behavior is clearly not acceptable in an academic setting and needs to be addressed in a professional manner. However, always remember that the invective is being directed at your *functional role*, not at you as a person. Letting your feelings dictate your actions will almost certainly lead to irrational and potentially embarrassing behavior on your part and end up wasting your time. When analyzing and attempting to solve problems, be rational, not emotional.

Working with Students

A typical department chair will spend a significant chunk of time interacting with students on a one-on-one basis. A major time management issue for a chair to consider is deciding which types of student interactions are appropriate for the chair to engage in and which should be delegated to other faculty or staff such as a department adviser. Which interactions should be delegated depends on the department's resources—for example, does the department have the resources to hire a department adviser or give one or more faculty release time to perform student advising? Regardless of how student matters are being delegated, it is often the case that students don't know where to go, and the chair is the natural go-to person if students don't know where else to go. Although an open-door policy for students may cast the chair as welcoming and friendly, it can also be a major drain on the chair's time. I suggest, if possible, having all students check in with a secretary or receptionist before knocking on the door to the chair's office. That way, the student can be directed to the appropriate person or to set up an appointment, depending on the nature of the student's question or concern. Let's take a look at some particular groups of students that many department chairs interact with and how to manage time with each group.

Counseling Current and Prospective Majors and Minors

A department's budget and general health often depend on the number of majors and minors declared in its programs. Student recruitment is an important matter in every department I know of, and although recruitment should be the responsibility of the whole department, it is often up to the chair to lead such efforts. For departments that serve a large number of majors, hiring a dedicated student recruiter would significantly reduce the time burden on the chair. The number of majors in a department as well as the extent to which the department is "hurting for students" may dictate the extent to which a chair may be directly involved with current and prospective majors. In my case, it was a top priority for my department to recruit and retain majors; I therefore instructed the front desk to sent every new major directly to me before the person was assigned a department adviser. I also made it a priority to talk to current majors if there was an issue that the assigned adviser could not deal with immediately.

Helping Students with Enrollment Issues

Students are quite sensitive to the fact that if they cannot enroll in a particular course that is required for graduation, this extends the time to graduation and increases the cost of their education.

For example, students who are unable to get into a class or section that has reached capacity have a legitimate concern that needs to be promptly addressed by the department chair or his or her designee. When we accept a student into an academic program, we have a responsibility to ensure that the courses the student needs to take are offered with reasonable frequency and ample capacity. One possible way to accommodate students with critical needs in a time-effective manner is to create a buffer for each class section by setting the maximum enrollment slightly lower than actual capacity. When this maximum is reached, students are placed on a waiting list, and the department chair or course instructor will decide who has the most critical need to make up the remaining capacity. Most institutions automatically favor students with the greatest needs by having students register for classes in order of seniority.

Long-term planning of course offerings is also essential to avoid wasting time fixing a constantly broken schedule. Many time conflicts can be avoided through better long-term planning. Whenever possible, it helps to have courses offered on a consistent basis year after year. This makes course planning less time-consuming, and if a time conflict has been resolved in one year, it is likely that it has been resolved for future years as well. Creating schedules that are consistent from year to year, however, is effective only if other departments that your students are taking courses from do the same. Unfortunately, many departments start by assigning instructors to courses and then allowing each instructor to decide independently when the course is to be offered. This often results in a scheduling nightmare both for the department offering the course and for the other departments affected as well.

As a statistician and department chair, I was always particularly concerned about collecting data on past enrollment trends and using these to project future needs for course offerings. However, you do not have to be a statistician to construct such projections. With a simple spreadsheet, you can use rolling averages of past enrollment to project future enrollment and estimate the number of sections needed given the maximum capacity available for each section.

Another problem arises when a student needs to take a class that has a time conflict with another class. Puzzles of this type can be extremely time-consuming to resolve. When you change the time of a course in order to resolve a time conflict, you inevitably create time conflicts for other students. If you must attempt to resolve a time conflict, I recommend that you first delegate to your secretary or assistant the responsibility to contact all of the students involved to identify the number of students with conflicts and alternative time slots available. For each time conflict, also have your assistant identify the course that it is conflicting with and a point of contact (department chair or instructor) if the course is not offered by your own department. With this information at hand, you are in a better position to negotiate with another department to change the time of its course if that should be necessary.

Sometimes a student's difficulty in enrolling in a course is a direct consequence of poor planning or choices on the student's part. For example, the student may have failed to register in a timely manner or failed to seek planning advice from an academic adviser. In such cases, it may be quite reasonable to have the student bear the negative consequences of his or her choices.

Advising Students with Instructor or Course Issues

Dealing with students (and parents) who have an issue with a particular instructor or course can be a major drain on a department chair's time and energy. Many faculty members I have spoken with over the years have cited this responsibility as the main reason for not wanting to serve as a department chair. I must admit that this was never my favorite responsibility either, but having been chair of a mathematics department with many frustrated students, I have ultimately become rather good at handling student complaints. Again, I want to reemphasize the comment I made earlier about the importance of separating the person you are from the position you hold.

When handling student complaints, I recommend that you set aside a time when you can comfortably listen to the student's concerns without interruption. If a student comes to you upset—say, over an incident that just happened in class—give the student a minute or two (at most) to summarize the problem and then have the student set up an appointment with you. If the student wants the problem dealt with here and now, you should say something like this: "It sounds to me that you have a serious issue, and I appreciate your bringing it to my attention. I need to make sure that I can devote my full attention to listening to your concerns; unfortunately, right now I have other things to attend to. So let's discuss it on . . ." and state the day and time. Delaying the conversation with the student gives you two advantages: the student will have had time to calm down, and you will have had an opportunity to discuss the matter with the instructor before meeting with the student.

Dealing with Students Charged with Misconduct or Violations of Academic Integrity

Dealing with students in this category may present many of the same challenges as the students discussed in the preceding section. In this case, the instructor rather than the student is the one that typically initiates the complaint. Fortunately, most institutions have well-established policies and procedures when it comes to handling issues involving plagiarism, cheating, and other student misconduct, and usually there are administrators and staff specifically assigned the responsibility of handling such issues. My best advice for department chairs is to be fully aware of all such policies and limit conversations with students and faculty involved to explaining each party's rights and responsibilities and providing a referral to the proper campus office or official.

Taking Care of Your Own Students

Department chairs generally have either the option or the requirement to teach courses in addition to their regular chair responsibilities. Most chairs are privileged to be able to teach courses they greatly enjoy, and being able to spend an hour or more of uninterrupted time in a classroom is often seen as a pleasant alternative to the many fragmented responsibilities of a department chair. As a chair and professor, it was my experience that the students in my own classes presented less challenging issues for me to deal with than those I dealt with as department chair.

However, the application of time management techniques is necessary to ensure that the courses and students you teach get the attention they deserve without unduly interfering with your other responsibilities. To accomplish this, I recommend blocking out times on your calendar not only for your scheduled classes but also for class preparation and grading as well as office hours specifically intended for your own students. If your office is not a place where you can easily work uninterrupted, you may want to consider scheduling times outside of your office, perhaps at home, to work on your class preparation.

The time spent on teaching activities by a department chair varies greatly from institution to institution, depending on the size and complexity of the department. Although teaching loads may be guided by institutional policies, it is always worthwhile to consider whether an appropriate balance exists between teaching and other chair duties. Is the time spent teaching preventing more important chair duties from getting done? If so, you may want to discuss with your dean or department if a reduction in your teaching responsibilities would be beneficial. When I first became department chair, I taught two courses during the regular school year with the option to teach a course during the summer period. As my department grew and requirements for paperwork from the administration became more and more demanding, I negotiated with my dean to reduce my teaching responsibilities, and in my last several years of being chair, I taught one course during the summer and no courses during the regular school year.

Questions to Consider and Practical Tips

- If you have access to it, review the data on your department's faculty searches (tenure track) conducted over the past two decades. What percentage of your searches resulted in a failed search, and what percentage of the faculty hired are still in your department? What are some of the common factors that contributed to faculty resigning or not earning tenure? How can you make a difference as a chair?

- Perform an inventory analysis of your faculty as described in this chapter. What are each person's strengths and weaknesses, preferences and dislikes? Are workload and resources distributed optimally, making maximum use of each person's strengths and making weaknesses irrelevant? Who among your faculty are the high achievers, and who perform less well? What influence do you have in motivating your low achievers to perform at higher levels?

- Revisit a recent conflict you had with a faculty member or between two faculty members that you helped resolve. In hindsight, could this conflict have been avoided or resolved in a more time-effective manner? Was each party given the opportunity to understand the perspective of the opposite party?

- Of all the types of student interactions discussed in this chapter, which demand most of your time? Could any of these be delegated to a faculty adviser?

- Does the number of courses you teach (if any) represent a reasonable teaching load given the workload associated with your regular chair duties? If not, what options do you have for reducing your teaching load or the number of chair duties—for example, by delegating more of these to your faculty and staff?

9

MANAGING UP AND OUT

Administration and External Relations

> The key to successful leadership today is influence, not authority.
>
> —*Kenneth Blanchard*

Department chairs serve as the interface between the faculty and the college or university administration. Although the job description of a department chair overlaps both with that of an administrator and that of a faculty member, most department chairs think of themselves as faculty members with administrative responsibilities rather than as administrators with faculty responsibilities (Gmelch and Miskin, 2004). The relationship between faculty and the administration is problematic at many campuses. Often faculty members have lost faith in their administration due to the perception that administrators are making decisions without adequate input from faculty, while administrators often perceive faculty as disgruntled people who frequently complain about decisions but at the same time fail to provide constructive input when given the opportunity. Bridging the communication gap between faculty and administration is yet another difficult and time-consuming task for the department chair that requires effective strategy and time management.

Working with the Dean

During my tenure as department chair, I had the pleasure of working with two different deans, with whom I developed fruitful and trustworthy working relationships. Seeing that the dean is your primary interface with the administration, a strong relationship between you and your dean is necessary for your personal success as well as that of your department. As suggested by the quotation opening this chapter, your department's success is dependent on your ability to influence your dean to make decisions in your department's favor. Doing so requires that you establish a high level of trust with your dean by exemplifying strong work ethics, dependability, and complete openness and honesty. Never attempt to hide or misrepresent information to your dean. If, for example, in the process of justifying a new position you attempt to make your student enrollment look better than it is by using data that you know are outdated, you will be perceived as untrustworthy once your dean discovers the truth and are likely to be subjected to undue scrutiny and micromanagement from that point on. Conversely, if you and your dean have established a high level of trust, it is likely that he or she will adopt a more hands-off approach, trusting you to make decisions with little oversight.

In establishing an effective working relationship with your dean, it is important to understand your dean's preferred style of communication. Does your dean prefer to communicate by phone, e-mail, or in person? Is he or she an open-door person, or are you expected to make an appointment with the secretary before consulting with your dean on an issue or a proposal? Does your dean like discussing business informally, or does he or she expect business matters to be presented in writing? By adapting to your dean's style of communication, you are much more likely to engage in effective communication and make good use of both your time and your dean's.

So far in this book, I have focused on managing individual time as well as department time. Apart from saving yourself and your department time, you should also be concerned with how you can avoid wasting the time of your dean and perhaps other higher-level administrators. If it is unclear why that is important to you, think about how closely your department's budget is tied to your dean's ability to compete for the overall college funding. Any hour you can save your dean and anything you can do to make your dean's job easier will ultimately benefit your department. Because your dean is a very busy person, when interacting with him or her you must stay focused on the topic of importance to you and keep social interactions and discussions of less relevant topics to a minimum.

During negotiations with your dean, keep two things in mind. First, your dean was once a faculty member and most likely also a department chair at some point, and he or she understands the dynamics of your department and that arguments are usually based on a rather narrow focus. Second, your dean will apply a global perspective in considering your arguments. What matters is not only what your particular department's needs are but, even more important, how your department fills a need for the college or university. In a typical university climate where funds are tight, it is likely that other departments face challenges or hardships similar to yours. If your needs are in fact of higher importance than those of the other departments, it is up to you to make the case for this.

Some of your interactions with your dean may involve issues related to student complaints. This is an area where you have the opportunity to save your dean's time. Most deans don't have the time for or any interest in dealing with dissatisfied students directly. Often when students file complaints, they submit them to the highest level of authority—perhaps even to a president or vice-president—but most administrators will immediately defer such inquiries down through the chain of command. Consequently, in the event that a student files a complaint directly with your dean before contacting you, it is likely that the dean will contact you before discussing the matter with the student. If that is not the case and your dean attempts to resolve the problem without involving you, you have a serious communication problem that needs immediate attention. But in the more likely event that the dean defers a problem for you to handle, your best approach is to immediately contact the student to set up an appointment. Take care of the problem and report back to your dean that it has been taken care of. You will gain substantial respect from your dean when you consistently handle such problems without his or her involvement. If, by contrast, the student files a complaint with you that you are not able to address to the student's satisfaction, you should anticipate the student's bringing the concern to the next level. In this case, it is important that you brief your dean about the issue before the student makes contact. Let your dean know how you attempted to address the concerns and discuss whether further action is needed. In most cases, your dean will either support your decision or send the student back to you for further conversation.

Working with Other Administrators

A department chair typically works with administrators in various campus offices either with or without the college dean directly involved. Examples may include working with a dean of graduate studies, a dean of students, or even a vice-president or president. If your dean is not directly involved in these conversations, it would be wise for you to provide a brief report on the conversations to avoid your dean's feeling "left out of the loop." In such situations, less is more. Don't waste time writing a lengthy report that your dean may not have time to read anyway. An e-mail with a few lines describing the meeting you had or are about to have and ending with "Call if you need more details" will generally suffice.

Sometimes your department may be fortunate to have a top administrator, possibly your president or provost, attend a portion of your department meeting. This is usually a golden opportunity for your department to make a favorable impression, and so this is a meeting for which you should make time to prepare. Because such administrators generally have very busy schedules, you are lucky if you end up having 30 minutes with this person, so that time needs to be spent wisely. Do not be offended if these administrators consider their time worth more than the time available to you and your entire faculty collectively. They may show up earlier or later than the time they agreed to, and they will expect you to focus your attention on them as soon as they show up. Arrange your agenda so that you have routine matters to cover before the administrator shows up, and be prepared to set those aside immediately upon his or her arrival. Typically, a meeting with a president or provost will begin with a standard report from the administrator on the "state of the university" or something of that nature. Such reports rarely contain any information that is not readily available from the media, official newsletters, faculty senate reports, or other sources, but nevertheless you should be prepared to listen politely.

At some point during the meeting, you and your colleagues will have an opportunity to ask questions. It would be a mistake to allow this time to be used by anybody who wants to express frustration over a particular issue, on which the administrator may not have any direct influence. So rather than turning this into a venting session, prepare a list of questions ahead of time. Unless the visit occurred on very short notice, you will have had some time to prepare such a list of questions with input from your colleagues. This will allow you to maintain a positive tone even if there are issues for which your department has concerns. You may also want to use the opportunity to highlight some recent achievements in your department that the administrator may not be aware of. Be sure to end the meeting on a positive note by thanking the administrator for taking time to visit with you and, if appropriate, present a small gift such as a department T-shirt or coffee mug, to show your appreciation.

Working with Accreditation Agencies

Preparing documents for an upcoming accreditation visit or an internal or external program review is often a task that departments dread. There has been an increased focus on departmental accountability in recent years, and during lean times, there is always a need to identify ineffective programs for possible elimination.

Many review processes have become predominantly electronic, with most information provided via a portal. This has not necessarily made the job of faculty and the department chair any easier than in the old days when all documentation was submitted in hardcopy form. Avoid making yourself responsible for the clerical data entry. Assuming that you have someone in charge of maintaining the portal, you can concentrate on gathering the necessary information.

Start by preparing a list of all information needed for the review, and identify who will be responsible for gathering it and by what deadline. Collect all information in a generic electronic format, such as a Microsoft Word document. The person entering the information into the portal will be able to use the cut-and-paste function, as opposed to retyping everything, and you will be able to reuse or update this information in later reviews. If your only record of a review is a printout from the portal, you will find it very difficult to reuse it for a similar review later. For that reason, wait to enter anything into the portal until it has been completely finalized in a generic form.

If the review process involves meeting with a group of reviewers, such a meeting should be taken very seriously. Don't underestimate what is at stake during the review. Come prepared to answer questions about your programs, and put your best foot forward in making a favorable impression on the reviewers. If there are questions that you cannot easily answer on the spot, write them down and let the reviewers know that you will get back to them promptly.

Once the review has been completed, there is a natural temptation to simply give a big sigh of relief and forget all about it until the next review comes around. Given the amount of time you have invested in this process, however, that would be a huge mistake. As you receive the final report of the reviewer, it would be a good idea to discuss the results with your colleagues and make note of both the strengths and weaknesses highlighted in the report. Discuss plans for rectifying any noted deficiencies well ahead of the next upcoming review.

Working with Local Schools and Businesses

Most academic departments have a mission that involves preparing graduates to be productive citizens in their local community, including schools, businesses, government agencies, and nonprofit organizations. Knowing what particular skills are demanded for the next generation of professionals in your community is vital to the success of your graduates, and such information is usually best attained through effective networking. For prestigious colleges and universities that seek to place their graduates more globally than locally, networking with the local community is equally important because such relationships strengthen the university through grants, research collaborations, and internship opportunities for students. Many larger departments have faculty and staff hired specifically to handle community outreach responsibilities, whereas in small departments it is often up to the department chair to pursue such relationships. Too many department chairs give a low priority to networking among the many tasks that demand their time and attention every day.

As with everything else that is important and not urgent, it takes dedicated effort to plan such activities. If your department's presence in the community has left room for improvement, you may want to take some time to discuss this with your colleagues and perhaps start by creating a list of schools or businesses with which you would like to establish a closer relationship. Of course, you can only do so much with your own time, and such activities may not bear fruit unless several of your faculty colleagues are also willing to make time for these actions. To encourage that, you may need to consider how these activities will benefit not only your department as a whole but also each faculty member. For example, are outreach activities considered in individual faculty activity plans and criteria for promotion and tenure? Outreach activities are generally both demanding and time-consuming, but often they offer no reward for the individual faculty member. Clearly, you cannot expect a faculty member to put tenure and promotion at risk by doing outreach activities if publication activity is the only major criterion used in the promotion process. If placing emphasis on outreach in faculty activity plans is not an option, what other incentives can you offer individual faculty members? The potential for being nominated for a service award may carry some weight with faculty members, but a reduction in teaching load or a summer stipend would be more significant for most faculty members.

Questions to Consider and Practical Tips

- What is your dean's preferred style of communication? If you had a significant request to present to your dean, such as a request for a new position, what would be the most effective way to present this request initially: a memo, a phone call, an e-mail, or a face-to-face meeting?

- Do you have a good relationship with the university's senior administration? Are the university's top officials aware of outstanding achievements your department has made recently? Would this be a good time to invite a provost or president to attend one of your department meetings?

- Make a timeline of regularly recurring program reviews and accreditation visits. Be proactive: delegate someone to gather the information that will be required ahead of time, and have that information put into generic electronic format.

- How is your relationship with local schools and businesses (whichever is more applicable to your discipline)? Would it be a good use of your department time for you or one of your colleagues to plan a visit to a local school or business in the near future or to invite one of their leaders to come to campus to meet with you?

10

A FINE BALANCE

Managing Work-Life Balance

> Every man dies. Not every man really lives.
> —William Wallace in the movie *Braveheart*

Due to the volume of tasks competing for department chairs' time, many chairs find themselves overwhelmed by the workload associated with the position, and especially in their first year, many chairs have trouble finding a balance between professional and personal commitments. Long working days is the rule for many chairs. Surveys reported in Gmelch and Burns (1993) identify "heavy workload" as the most commonly cited source of stress for department chairs. And many additional hours are spent thinking about difficult decisions coming up or worrying about how to get everything done.

Where should we draw the line between being a workaholic and simply being a dedicated chair who greatly cares about the success of the department? MacKenzie (1997) makes the interesting observation that workaholics are addicted to *work* rather than to *results*. Workaholics work simply for work's sake, and in spite of the many hours they put in, they tend not to make a major impact in their organization. Workaholism is closely related to the "urgency addiction" we discussed in Chapter Two, a destructive habit that like other addictions may lead to personal problems such as broken relationships and alienated children (MacKenzie, 1997).

When asked what is most important to them, many people cite family relationships and personal health. Yet when you

120

analyze how the same people spend and prioritize their time, the tasks and activities necessary to nourish personal health and family relationships often get compromised due to demanding work-related activities. We all know the symptoms. When things get busy at work, exercise, family time, sleep, and healthy nutrition are usually the first to suffer. This behavior, however, is inconsistent with the "big rocks" principle referred to numerous times in this book. Buller (2010a) suggests, "Rather than scheduling your work and allowing exercise, sleep, time with family or friends, leisurely meals and intellectual or spiritual activities to fill in your down time, these essential pursuits should be blocked out on your calendar before anything else is scheduled."

So you may wonder how many hours per week it is reasonable to expect a department chair to work while keeping a healthy balance between professional and personal priorities. The answer will of course vary from person to person, and it is perhaps not even an appropriate question to ask to begin with. Perhaps a more appropriate question is, How many hours are *available* for work after the priorities related to personal health and family commitments have been met? Rather than asking how you can fit exercise and family activities into your work schedule, ask yourself how you can best accomplish required work functions in the time remaining after you have taken care of all your higher-ranking priorities.

Because you have only a fixed number of hours available to split between your professional and personal priorities, taking proper care of personal priorities that you are currently ignoring may result in an overall reduction in the number of hours you work. Efforts to reduce the number of hours you are working should not be abused, but there is nothing wrong with working 40 hours a week if you are maximally productive during each of those hours. Imagine what you could accomplish if you could be as effective with your time as you are when teaching a class: realizing that there is always far more material to cover than you can manage in a 50-minute period, you focus on the most essential items, the stuff you *must* cover. When it is time to go, it is time to go. Your students won't hang around if you go over your allotted time. Why should you do that to yourself?

Covey (2004b) speaks to the importance of maintaining and renewing our four intelligences:

- Physical intelligence (PQ): physical exercise, proper nutrition and sleep
- Mental intelligence (IQ): mental exercise, reading
- Emotional intelligence (EQ): nurturing friendships, social relationships
- Spiritual intelligence (SQ): developing personal values, service, leaving a legacy

Although many of the activities necessary to exercise these four intelligences are performed in one's personal time, some of these are also work-related activities. For example, engaging in stimulating and challenging scholarly activity is clearly an IQ activity, and developing the social climate in your department is an EQ activity.

The four intelligences listed are connected with each of the four parts—body, mind, heart, and spirit—that make up what Covey (2004b) refers to as the "whole person" paradigm. The number of hours per week it takes to exercise the "whole body" again varies from person to person. Some people may function well with six hours of sleep while others may require eight hours. Some families, such as those with young children or teenagers at home or those that include an elderly parent to care for, demand a lot of time. Many people find it hard to set aside five hours per week for physical exercise, yet according to some surveys, the average American spends in excess of 30 hours per week sitting in front of a television or pursuing other passive entertainment that contributes little to the exercise of any of the four intelligences.

Another factor in determining how many hours are available for work is the distinction between normal instruction days and days when classes are not in session. A typical college or university will have approximately 160 days of instruction during the regular academic year (including exam periods), whether it is on a quarter or semester system. Regardless of the teaching load, those days will typically be the most demanding for a department chair, but they account for less than half the days in the calendar year. Although noninstructional days are not considered vacation, even for regular faculty, those are generally the days when a department chair has some flexibility in how many hours to work and also good days for fitting in the "big rocks" related to the four intelligences that often get neglected during the busy periods. As mentioned in Chapter Four, when creating a time budget and in keeping a time log, it is appropriate to differentiate between instructional and noninstructional days.

Finally, I want to emphasize salary or compensation, or more particularly disposable income, as a factor in how many hours are available for a department chair to work. It is generally recognized that department chairs are not adequately compensated for the extra time they are expected to put in, and surveys also suggest that almost no chairs originally choose this career path for the prospect of additional compensation (Gmelch and Miskin, 2004). Regardless of salary, however, as result of the recent economic downturn, the general trend of increases in the cost of living without matching increases in salary has caused a reduction in the disposable income of many department chairs. This is a factor because the chairs with more disposable income have better ability to outsource many of the chores that others end up doing themselves, such as those related to home maintenance and home improvement projects.

Taking Time Management Home with You

Many people, even people who frequently bring work home with them, are reluctant to apply time management techniques in their personal lives. I will not go into detail on the need for or appropriateness of bringing work home with you; rather I will focus on the need to bring the time management tools home with you when you leave the office. For most department chairs, the line between work and personal life is fuzzy at best; fortunately, it is not necessary for a department chair to maintain a rigid 8:00-to-5:00 daily work schedule or to leave computers and planners at the office to maintain a healthy work-life balance. One of the most common misconceptions among people reluctant to adopt time management in their personal lives is that it will take away freedom or not allow for spontaneous behavior (MacKenzie, 1997). Hence the paradox that many successful professionals put great effort into managing their time effectively while at work only to go home and waste dozens of hours of valuable personal time. The truth is that time management allows for *more* freedom and spontaneous behavior, at the same time allowing us to spend more time on things we enjoy doing, such as spending time with our families, hobbies, reading, or simply relaxing.

Almost all of the time management techniques that have been discussed in this book can and should be applied in your personal life as well as in your professional life. Shouldn't your personal goals, such as developing satisfying relationships and raising educated and responsible children, rank at least as high as the professional goals we build our daily priorities around? Applying time management does not mean that you let a to-do list or a 24-hour calendar run your life or that you must keep a log of every minute that you spend every day. Time management is about developing priorities consistent with your most important values and planning your activities around those priorities. Some people prefer to keep separate to-do lists and calendars for professional and personal business, an approach that I strongly recommend *against*. That is because almost nobody's time is strictly divided into professional and personal time. Doctor's appointments and kids' sports and school activities often occur in the middle of a weekday, and professional commitments such as an open house or a university event often take place on week-ends. Not knowing which of the two calendars to consult can be a constant source of human error, and people with multiple cal-endars are much more likely to miss appointments or schedule conflicting appointments. For the to-do list, it is good practice to categorize (perhaps even color-code) tasks and activities to distinguish professional and personal items. This makes it easy to sort and prioritize tasks quickly, whether you are planning your regular workday or an upcoming weekend or holiday.

As with your professional time, when you waste time in your personal life, you prevent yourself from achieving the goals that are most important to you. Identifying time wasters in your per-sonal life is a means of gaining more space for such things as leisure activities you wish you had more time for. For example, do you waste time because of lack of planning or personal disor-ganization? Are you inefficient at delegating, say, by involving your children in home chores that you end up doing yourself or by failing to hire people to do tasks that you are currently doing who can perform them at a much lower hourly rate than your own? Do you have trouble saying no to other people's requests for activities that take up your time and prevent you from pursu-ing your own priorities?

Winning the Time Lottery

I now invite you to participate in a self-reflective thought experi-ment that I often introduce to participants when conducting time management workshops for department chairs (Hansen, 2007, 2009b). Imagine a hypothetical situation in which you are noti-fied that you had won the "time lottery." Every day for the rest of your life, you are given an extra hour to spend any way you like. Write down one or more tasks or activities that you would either start doing or spend more time doing with that extra time.

Now imagine another hypothetical situation in which for the rest of your life you had one less hour every day. (This could even come to pass if, for instance, you develop a medical condition that requires an hour's treatment each day or you must spend an hour caring for a family member.) Write down which tasks and activities you are currently doing that you would stop doing or do less of.

Compare the tasks and activities you identified in each part of this exercise. Are they different? If so, are the ones you would do more of more or less important than the ones you would do less of? If more important, what is stopping you from simply swapping the two lists, that is, stop doing the items on the second list and start doing the ones on the first list?

Through my interactions with department chairs, I have learned that the first list often includes such tasks and activities as sleeping, spending time with spouse and family, exercising, reading, getting organized, and hobbies. The second list often includes such items as checking e-mail, attending unproductive meetings, doing tasks that could be delegated, responding to other people's priorities, and socializing or chitchatting.

The theme here is that if we had less time, we would be forced to use our time more effectively by eliminating time wasters. But if we had more time, we would not want to just waste it. We would spend more time on things that are important to us, but because they are not urgent, we don't do them or we don't do enough of them. The reality is that for most of us, simply swapping the two lists would be practically as good as winning the "time lottery."

Managing Your Stress

The literature on time management and stress management overlap in many of the topics discussed. Common themes mentioned in both include personal health, wellness, and organization; quality of human relationships; and the sense of making a difference in other people's lives (building a legacy). Some authors believe that time and stress management are related in that being good at managing your time will lead to good stress management as well. MacKenzie (1997) notes that "time management is stress management at its highest level" (p. 16). Other authors believe that the relationship between time management and stress is more complex. Buller (2010a) notes that "the more productive many people are, the more tense and anxious they may feel, and demands are increased in proportion to their improved efficiency" (p. 16). Conversely, being able to manage stress alone is not necessarily an indicator of good time management. Anyone who has raised teenagers is likely to have seen people with low stress who are not good at managing their time. Gmelch and Miskin (2004) discuss the importance of achieving just the right level of stress. I like to think of an analogy of achieving the right level of stress being similar to running an engine at its ideal operating temperature. When our level of stress is too low (like a cool engine), we are not operating effectively. We lack adequate challenge and are at risk of boredom and "rust-out." At the other end of the scale, if our level of stress is too high (like an overheating engine), we are equally ineffective. With a high level of stress comes fatigue and increased risk of human error and "burnout" as result. Buller (2010b) suggests that one of the tools for managing stress is to turn the negative aspects of stress into something positive by making stress your "ally." However, this cannot be accomplished in isolation but must be achieved through a series of stress reduction techniques that include managing our basic health, focusing on the present, creating awareness of our environment, and making use of our academic and administrative resources. Many of these techniques again represent various exercises of our four intelligences.

Claiming Your Reward for a Job Well Done

I hope that this book has provided you with some practical tips on how you can begin to make changes that will enable you to achieve more with your limited time. Once you have adopted the right set of time management tools and habits, the benefits for your academic institution will be evident, even if you end up spending fewer hours at work. Your colleagues will know that they can count on you when you make a commitment to them and respect you when you say no. Your staff will feel more appreciated when you delegate tasks to them with stewardship and authority and when you acknowledge them for their contributions and results. You will avoid dictating methods or wasting your time doing other people's work. You will manage your stress and be in a better position to handle the crises that you have to deal with from time to time.

Having achieved the goal of being highly effective, now is the time to reward yourself. Spend some of your extra time with your loved ones, and set aside time to do more of the things that you really enjoy. Likewise, should you start slipping back into old and ineffective behaviors and habits such as procrastination and lack of planning and organization, the punishment you receive is spending more long hours at work, paying back the hours you wasted. As you become more aware of your own effectiveness, you will feel the motivation to give the new habits another try, even if you fail to use them. And when you do fail to use them, don't worry; we are all entitled to make mistakes some of the time. Appreciate your mistakes as opportunities for continued learning. As John Enoch Powell said, "The only real mistake is the one from which we learn nothing."

Questions to Consider and Practical Tips

- If you completed the time lottery exercise in this chapter, compare your two lists side by side. For the next week, try trading one activity from your second list (something you are currently doing) with one from your first list (something you are not currently doing).

- Review your time budget from Chapter Four, or create one if you have not already done so. Identify the hours budgeted to exercising each of the four intelligences discussed in this chapter. Are you getting sufficient exercise for each part of your "whole person" to achieve balance between professional and personal priorities?

- Reexamine a recent stressful task or activity performed as part of your department chair duties, such as resolving a conflict or completing a task under a tight deadline. Analyze how you accomplished the task in terms of academic and administrative resources you used. Is it possible to use this experience positively in preparing for a future challenge of similar nature, using stress as your ally rather than your enemy?

- Estimate the hours you have saved recently by applying good time management techniques. Give yourself a reward for a job well done!

References

Allen, D. *Getting Things Done: The Art of Stress-Free Productivity*. New York: Viking, 2001.

Bialozor, B., and Bialozor, W. "Just in Time: Effective Use of Departmental Meetings." *Proceedings of the 23rd K-STATE Academic Chairpersons Conference*, 2006.

Bond, W. J. *199 Time-Waster Situations and How to Avoid Them*. Hollywood, Fla.: Fell, 1991.

Buller, J. L. *The Essential Department Chair: A Practical Guide to College Administration*. Bolton, Mass.: Anker, 2006.

Buller, J. L. "Coping with the Stress of Higher Education Administration: A Holistic Approach, Part One." *Department Chair*, 2010a, *21*(1), 15–17.

Buller, J. L. "Coping with the Stress of Higher Education Administration: A Holistic Approach, Part Two." *Department Chair*, 2010b, *21*(2), 10–12.

Chu, D. *The Department Chair Primer*. Bolton, Mass.: Anker, 2006.

Conway, J. B. *On Being a Department Head: A Personal View*. Providence, R.I.: American Mathematical Society, 1996.

Cooper, A. *Alice Cooper, Golf Monster: A Rock 'n' Roller's 12 Steps to Becoming a Golf Addict*. New York: Crown, 2007.

Covey, S. *The Seven Habits of Highly Effective People*. New York: Fireside, 1989.

Covey, S. "Big Rocks," 2004a. http://www.YouTube.com (keywords: covey big rocks)

Covey, S. *The Eighth Habit: From Effectiveness to Greatness*. New York: Free Press, 2004b.

Covey, S., Merrill, A., and Merrill, R. *First Things First: Coping with the Ever-Increasing Demands of the Workplace*. New York: Free Press, 1994.

Crandell, G. "Time Management for More Effective Results." *Department Chair*, 2005, *15*(3), 11–12.

Dobbins, R., and Pettman, B. O. "Creating More Time." *Equal Opportunities International*, 1998, *17*(2), 18–27.

Douglass, M. E., and Douglass, D. N. *Manage Your Time, Manage Your Work, Manage Yourself.* New York: AMACOM, 1980.

Douglass, M. E., and Douglass, D. N. *Manage Your Time, Your Work, Yourself.* New York: AMACOM, 1993.

Fiore, N. A. *The Now Habit: A Strategic Program for Overcoming Procrastination and Enjoying Guilt-Free Play.* New York: Penguin, 2006.

Gmelch, W. H. "Choosing the Path of Academic Leadership: How to Survive and Stay Alive." *Proceedings of the 21st K-STATE Academic Chairpersons Conference,* 2004.

Gmelch, W. H., and Burns, J. S. "The Cost of Academic Leadership: Department Chair Stress." *Innovative Higher Education,* 1993, *17*(4), 259–270.

Gmelch, W. H., and Miskin, V. D. *Chairing an Academic Department* (2nd ed.). Madison, Wis.: Atwood, 2004.

Hansen, C. K. "Effective Time Management for Academic Leaders." *Proceedings of the 24th K-STATE Academic Chairpersons Conference,* 2007.

Hansen, C. K. "Taking Control of Your Time: A Guide to Effective Time Management." *Academic Leader,* 2008, *24*(6), 1, 6, 8.

Hansen, C. K. "Technology Trends in Mobile Communication: How Mobile Are Your Data?" *IEEE Reliability Society Annual Technology Report,* 2009a. http://paris.utdallas.edu/IEEE-RS-ATR/

Hansen, C. K. "Time Management: Getting the Job Done and More Time to Play." *Proceedings of the 26th K-STATE Academic Chairpersons Conference,* 2009b.

Hecht, I. "Time Management: The Chair's Challenge." *Department Chair,* 2005, *15*(4), 3–4.

Hecht, I., Higgerson, M. L., Gmelch, W. H., and Tucker, A. *The Department Chair as Academic Leader.* Phoenix, Ariz.: Oryx Press, 1999.

Hedges, J. "A Time Management Exercise for Faculty Meetings." *Department Chair,* 2003, *14*(2), 8–10.

Higgerson, M. L. *Communication Skills for Department Chairs.* Bolton, Mass.: Anker, 1996.

Hochel, S., and Wilson, C. E. *Hiring Right: Conducting Successful Searches in Higher Education.* San Francisco: Jossey-Bass, 2007.

Koch, R. *The 80/20 Principle.* New York: Doubleday, 1998.

Lakein, A. *How to Get Control of Your Time and Your Life.* New York: Wyden, 1973.

Leamyng, D. R. *Academic Leadership. A Practical Guide to Chairing the Department* (2nd ed.). Bolton, Mass.: Anker, 2007.

Lees, N. D. *Chairing Academic Departments. Traditional and Emerging Expectations.* Bolton, Mass.: Anker, 2006.

Leland, K., and Bailey, K. *Time Management in an Instant: 60 Ways to Make the Most of Your Day.* Franklin Lakes, N.J.: Career Press, 2008.

MacKenzie, A. *The Time Trap* (3rd ed.). New York: AMACOM, 1997.

MacKenzie, A., and Nickerson, P. *The Time Trap* (4th ed.). New York: AMACOM, 2009.

Morgenstern, J. *Time Management from the Inside Out: The Foolproof System for Taking Control of Your Schedule—and Your Life* (2nd ed.). New York: Henry Holt/Owl Books, 2004.

Parkinson, C. N. "Parkinson's Law." *Economist*, Nov. 19, 1955.

Pausch, R. "Time Management," 2008. http://www.YouTube.com (keywords: pausch time management)

Robinson, J. P., and Godbey, G. *Time for Life: The Surprising Ways Americans Use Their Time* (2nd ed.). University Park: Pennsylvania State University Press, 1999.

Tucker, A. *Chairing the Academic Department. Leadership Among Peers* (3rd ed.). Phoenix, Ariz.: Oryx Press, 1992.

Whisenhunt, D. W. *Administrative Time Management: Tips for Administrators and Aspiring Administrators.* Lanham, Md.: University Press of America, 1987.

Index

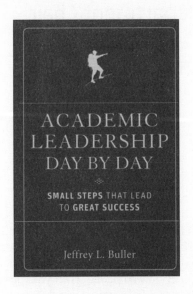

Academic Leadership Day by Day

Small Steps That Lead to Great Success

by Jeffrey L. Buller

978-0-470-90300-1
Cloth | 336 p
US$ 25.00 | CAN$ 28.00

"This book is practical, insightful, and immediately useful. It should be on the desk—and within easy reach—of every academic leader." —**Peter Seldin**, distinguished professor of management, Pace University; coauthor, *The Administrative Portfolio: A Practical Guide to Improved Administrative Performance and Personnel Decisions*

"I'm always impressed by Jeff Buller's ability to cut through jargon and gimmicks to give academic leaders the sort of advice they can really use. There are more good ideas on a single page of this book than in entire volumes many times its size."—**Walt Gmelch**, dean and professor, School of Education, University of San Francisco; author, *The Seasons of a Dean's Life*

Academic Leadership Day by Day takes an entirely different approach to developing your proven academic leadership: It introduces one practical and field-tested idea each day for an entire academic year. Rather than requiring you to devote days or even weeks to administrative training (which may prove to be of little use in the end), this manual gives you no-nonsense suggestions that you can consider on even your busiest days. Experiment with the suggestions made each day, discover what works for you, and then build on your successes for the benefit of your institution and its programs. Significant improvements often result from small, gradual, and consistent efforts, and *Academic Leadership Day by Day* is your guide to becoming a more accomplished, confident academic leader a few minutes at a time.

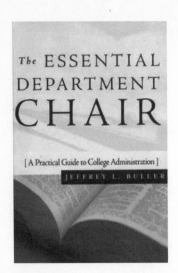

The Essential
Department Chair
A Practical Guide to
College Administration

by Jeffrey Buller

978-1-882982-99-8
Paper | 312 p
US$ 40.00 | CAN$ 43.99

This book is the quintessential manual for what department chairs must know to excel at the many administrative tasks assigned to them on a day-to-day basis. For instance, how do you cultivate a potential donor for much-needed departmental resources? How do you interview someone when your dean assigns you to a committee searching for an administrator in a different academic area? How do you fire someone? How do you get your department members to work together more harmoniously? How do you keep the people who report to you motivated and capable of seeing the big picture?

This book is about the "how" of academic administration. Based on a series of workshops given by the author in the area of faculty and administrative development, each topic deals concisely with the most important information chairs will want to have at their fingertips when faced with a particular challenge or opportunity. Intended to be a ready reference that chairs turn to as needed, this book emphasizes proven solutions and stresses what chairs need to know now in order to be most successful in their administrative positions.

Jeffrey L. Buller is vice president for academic affairs and dean of the college at Mary Baldwin College. He began his administrative career as honors director and chair of the Department of Classical Studies at Loras College in Dubuque, Iowa, before going on to assume a series of administrative appointments at Georgia Southern University. Dr. Buller has published widely on Greek and Latin literature, Wagnerian music drama, and higher education administration, including a large number of articles that have appeared in *The Department Chair*.

The Academic Chair's Handbook

By Daniel W. Wheeler, Alan T. Seagren, Linda Wysong Becker, Edward R. Kinley, Dara D. Mlinek, and Kenneth J. Robson

978-0-470-19765-3
Cloth | 304 p
US$ 42.00 | CAN$ 45.99

"Every aspiring, new, and experienced chairperson will benefit from this rich resource of many integrated and well-tested strategies that foster faculty development and their own development."
—Larry A. Braskamp, professor emeritus, Loyola University Chicago

This second edition of *The Academic Chair's Handbook* provides an updated, comprehensive, and practical guide for academic department chairs and division heads at both two- and four-year institutions. This essential resource includes new material on a variety of topics such as technology, funding and resources, departmental climate and quality, assessment, and accreditation, and describes several strategies department chairs can use to build a positive work environment that fosters professional growth of both faculty and chairs. The book's self-assessment inventory can help determine which strategy is most appropriate for a particular situation. While the strategies are upbeat, positive, and developmental, they clearly address the often harsh political realities involved in chairing academic departments.

Daniel W. Wheeler is professor and head of the Department of Agricultural Leadership, Education, and Communication at the University of Nebraska–Lincoln. **Alan T. Seagren** is professor emeritus and director of the Center for the Study of Higher and Postsecondary Education at the University of Nebraska–Lincoln. **Linda Wysong Becker** is vice president for student services at Union College in Lincoln, Nebraska. **Edward R. Kinley** is associate vice president for academic affairs and chief information officer at Indiana State University. **Dara D. Mlinek** is a former research assistant and instructor in the Center for the Study of Higher and Postsecondary Education at the University of Nebraska–Lincoln and participated in the research efforts focused on chairs. **Kenneth J. Robson** has served as a department chair, dean, and vice president. He is currently engaged in a higher education consulting practice with his partner J. Judith Eifert.

Jossey-Bass Department Chair Leadership Institute Online Seminar Series

www.departmentchairs.org

The Jossey-Bass Department Chair Leadership Institute is proud to offer practical, completely interactive 90-minute online sessions for department chairs. These seminars are designed to provide the professional enrichment, networking opportunities, and essential training that most department chairs never have the chance to experience but desperately need. The benefits include:

- You can attend from anywhere! Taking place completely over the Web, the seminar series is wherever you are. All sessions begin at 11:30 EST and all you need to participate is a computer with internet access.
- Enjoy access to recorded sessions for six months after the event. Can't attend the live date? No problem – you can review the content whenever it's most convenient for *you*.
- Interact with and learn directly from dynamic speakers and experts
- Receive complimentary resources plus special discounts on Jossey-Bass and Wiley books and periodicals – good for professional development titles *and* discipline-specific resources.
- Cost-effective pricing, early bird discounts, and zero travel make this one of the most economical professional development opportunities available to department chairs.
- Live interaction and networking with other department chairs and professionals, just like yourself!

For more information and to register, simply visit **www.departmentchairs.org**. While you're there, be sure to sign up for our free bi-monthly e-newsletter, *The Jossey-Bass Department Chair Insider*.